PRINCIPLES OF SEMIOTIC

PRINCIPLES OF SEMIOTIC

D. S. CLARKE

Routledge & Kegan Paul
London and New York

First published in 1987 by
Routledge & Kegan Paul Inc.
in association with Methuen Inc.
29 West 35th Street, New York, NY 10001

Published in the UK by
Routledge & Kegan Paul Ltd
11 New Fetter Lane, London EC4P 4EE

Set in Times New Roman
by Columns, Reading, Great Britain
and printed in Great Britain by
Richard Clay Ltd, Bungay, Suffolk

Library of Congress Cataloging in Publication Data
Clarke, D.S. (David S.), 1936—
Principles of semiotic.
Bibliography: p.
Includes index.
1. Semiotics. I. Title.
P99.C54   1987   401.41   86-21945

British Library CIP Data also available
ISBN 0-7102-0981-9 (cased)
ISBN 0-7102-1136-8 (pb)

TO MY TEACHER
CHARLES HARTSHORNE

CONTENTS

PREFACE

Semiotic has a long, continuous history that dates back to the debates between the Stoics and Epicureans over the status of the sign as an object of interpretation. Despite this history the present prospects for the subject in British and American philosophy seem very dim indeed. Interest in the subject in the English-speaking world is confined primarily to those either with historical interests or in fields such as literature, theatre, or film influenced by the tradition of European semiology (or 'cultural semiotics'), an area of study with a much different focus from that of past periods. This work is an attempt to reestablish semiotic on the basis of principles more consistent with its past history and especially with the guiding ideas found in the writings of Peirce and Morris. This task has been made easier by the work of such recent philosophers as Grice, Strawson, Austin, Bennett, and Lewis, who have introduced into current philosophy of language – often without explicitly acknowledging it – discussion of issues directly relevant to those of the Peirce-Morris tradition. It is because of this recent work and also because of advances in our understanding of sub-human systems of communication that the nature of semiotic as a discipline has changed and advanced beyond that defined forty years ago in the writings of Morris.

The book is divided into two parts, with the first two chapters providing the background for the more systematic discussions of signs at different levels taken up in the last three. Much of the interest in semiotic stems from the comparative insights it contributes to our understanding of language use. In the final chapter issues that have become the focus of recent philosophy of language regarding the reference, meaning, and truth of sentences are discussed in the light of the analogies to more primitive signs developed in the preceding two chapters. I have tried to make both background and systematic discussions accessible to a wide variety of readers, an introduction to what I conceive as the key issues of semiotic as a viable part of present-day philosophy. The notes to be found at the end are designed to inform those interested in the extensive literature on the subject and more specialized problems.

The origins of this work date back to studies of Peirce's semiotic and participation in seminars conducted by Charles Hartshorne in which he developed his philosophy of panpsychism – both of which took place while I was a graduate student at Emory University in the early 1960s. Hartshorne's vision of human experience being continuous with that found in all forms of life seemed to me then, and still does now, an exalted one, an essential correction to the anthropocentric bias of post-Cartesian philosophy. I was then swept up in his project of constructing a metaphysical system in which basic features of human experience, as basic as the substance, form, and matter distinctions of Aristotle, were to be extended to all sentient organisms. But the basis for this extension used by Hartshorne and the Whiteheadean tradition he represents seemed to me defective, one no longer viable in the face of the successful critiques of *a priori* psychologizing by the linguistic philosophers. Instead, the basis, I thought, must be our use and interpretation of language, with semiotic the means for extending their principal features. It is this revision which this work attempts to carry out.

I am very grateful for the help of students and faculty colleagues at Southern Illinois University with whom I have discussed these issues over the past few years. In particular, I owe much to the careful reading of an earlier manuscript version by Thomas Mitchell and Mark Johnson; both have provided valuable criticisms leading to revisions. I owe a similar debt to an anonymous reader for Routledge & Kegan Paul. To Stratford Caldecott I am grateful for encouragement and guidance in the early planning of the work. Part of its preparation was made possibly by a research grant from Southern Illinois University at Carbondale for the summer of 1985.

Carbondale, Illinois
December, 1985

1 INTRODUCTION

In contemporary philosophy the focus of study is the use and interpretation of language. To study scientific inquiry is to study the language of science and how it is used; to study legal decision-making is to study the language used in applying laws; to study aesthetic expression is to study the symbolic forms for this expression; and so it is for every human activity. For philosophy seeks to understand the nature of thought, and to think is to use and interpret language, sometimes as it is publicly expressed by ourselves and others, sometimes in the form of what Plato calls in the *Phaedo* the 'inner dialogue of the soul with itself' where public expression is suppressed or delayed. If we had special introspective powers by which we could directly intuit the nature of our thought processes, then language might play a less central role in philosophical investigations. But we have no such powers, and previous attempts to describe directly these processes and their contents through such terms as 'concept', 'idea', 'sense data', etc. can be shown to be in fact importing distinctions derived from language. Hence the shift instituted at the end of the nineteenth century by Frege and Peirce from a conception of philosophy as the study of psychological processes to one concentrating on the description and analysis of linguistic expressions.

On these points almost all can probably agree, and the justification for making the shift is generally accepted. Differences arise mainly over the method to be used in studying language and the objectives to be pursued. It is helpful at this preliminary stage to review briefly the two methods that have dominated recent philosophy in the English-speaking world and to raise some difficulties that confront them. This will help us to determine the special role semiotic can hope to play in relation to contemporary studies of language.

1

1.1 Logical analysis

Bertrand Russell can be credited with instituting the widely adopted method for applying the symbolism and paraphrase techniques of modern predicate logic to sentences in natural languages in order to clarify their meaning, and thereby correct philosophic conclusions based on a misunderstanding of their logical form. Russell's paradigm sentence, the one whose analysis can be regarded as starting the logical program, was

(1) The present king of France is bald
    which he paraphrased by

(2) Exactly one (material) thing is such that it is a king of France and bald

Its representation in symbolic notation becomes finally

(3) $\exists x[Kx \ \& \ \forall y(Ky \supset y=x) \ \& \ Bx]$

with 'K' for 'is a king of France' and 'B' for 'is bald'. In (3) the existential quantifier '$\exists x$' and the first two conjuncts within its scope have the effect of stating that there exists at least one king of France and at most one (any other thing which is a king of France will be identical with the one which has been stated to exist). The third conjunct as quantified states this king is bald. The effect of the paraphrase is to change the subject from the original grammatical subject 'the present king of France' in (1) to the general subject 'thing' or 'material thing' of (2). This latter is the logical subject, and is represented by the variable 'x' within the existential quantifier. The 'true' meaning of (1) is revealed, Russell claims, only by the paraphrase, and this meaning is represented by the sentence's logical form as (3).[1] The project of analysis begun by Russell was to be carried out by similarly paraphrasing and representing all those other sentences of ordinary language whose grammatical form disguised logical form in a way giving rise to philosophical confusions.

    The symbolism of formal logic was originally designed to represent the form of sentences within the context of inferences in order to evaluate these inferences as valid or invalid. In order to make such evaluations the logician must make certain assumptions. The most fundamental are those which insure a connection between the premisses and conclusion of a given inference. Consider an example of the simplest of all inferences,

(4) John is sitting

Therefore, John is sitting

in which the conclusion simply repeats the premiss. It is, of course, valid. But in order to establish its validity we must assume that the sentence 'John is sitting' as it occurs in the premiss expresses the same content in the conclusion. This common content necessary for validity is labelled the 'proposition' expressed by the two occurrences or tokens of the sentence. Sameness of proposition in turn requires first that what logicians call the 'denotation' of its subject term 'John' remains constant, i.e., that there be a unique individual which both occurrences of the name denote. And second, granted that we have the same proposition, we must assume its truth value remains constant, that if it is true in the premiss it remains true in the conclusion. John could stand up between the time a speaker utters the premiss and then utters the conclusion, and hence the premiss would be true and conclusion false. Logic must assume that this does not occur. The effect of these assumptions is to abstract the sentence 'John is sitting' as it occurs in the content of inference (4) from its use or interpretation by a person on a given occasion. All we need to know in evaluating (4) as valid is that *if* the premiss *were* true then the conclusion *would* be true also. For this a person's assertion of or assent to the sentence at a given time and place is irrelevant.

Outside inferential contexts, of course, sentences function very differently. On different occasions of use the name 'John' may be used by a speaker to refer to different individuals. The triadic relation between an utterance of a name within a sentence, a person using or interpreting the sentence, and a referent, is thus different from the dyadic relation between the name and what it uniquely denotes as considered by the logician for his special purposes of evaluating inferences (cf. below Section 5.2). And similarly for change of truth value. 'John is sitting' as used on one occasion can be asserted as true, while on another denied as false, contrary to what must be assumed when the sentence is used as a premiss and our task is inference evaluation.

It is small wonder, then, that Russell's project of employing techniques and symbolism designed for inferences where truth and denotation constancy are assumed, would encounter difficulties when applied to sentences isolated from inferential contexts. As Strawson has shown, it is because the assumptions do not generally hold of these sentences that Russell's paraphrase and representation of sentence (1) is defective.[2] To assert the proposition it expresses as true, or to assent to it, presupposes the existence of its referent on that occasion. Only if we can identify the referent of the singular term 'the present king of France' can we judge the proposition true or false. Since this condition does not hold (in fact, there is no such referent), (1) cannot be asserted or assented to. Yet (2) must be asserted as false, since its first conjunct as quantified falsely states there is at least one king of France.[3] Hence, (2) cannot be regarded as having the same logical meaning expressed in more perspicuous form as (1).

Implicit in Russell's project of analysis is the assumption that every sentence with a specific meaning has a unique logical form which paraphrase and logical representation can reveal. The meaning of a sentence is regarded as equivalent to the totality of consequences that it (or the proposition it expresses) logically entails. To specify a sentence's meaning then becomes the task of representing its form in such a way that the inferences to all these consequences can be shown to be valid. But, in fact, no one logical representation will justify this indefinite number of inferences. Consider, for example, Donald Davidson's analysis of action sentences such as

(5) John walks in the street

which Davidson proposes to paraphrase by 'There is an event which is such that John walks in it and it (the event) is in the street.' This is finally represented by

(6) $\exists x(Wjx \ \& \ Ixs)$

This is claimed to represent the form of (5), since it justifies the inference to its consequence 'John walks'.[4] Indeed, this inference is justified, but the cost in intuitive plausibility is a high one, since we are forced into introducing a variable ranging over events, names of individual things such as persons and things, and strange relations between them, e.g. the relation of walking in between John and an event. Moreover, there are other consequences which (6) will not justify, consequences such as 'John sometimes walks', 'John walks somewhere', and 'It is possible that John walks'. To represent them we will have to introduce additional variables ranging over other 'objects' such as times, places, and actual and possible worlds. Such objects require even more bizarre relations between them.

All of this seems to show that there is not some meaning of (5) which some unique logical form can specify. Instead, there is an indefinite variety of inferential contexts in which (5) can occur, and as these contexts vary we vary our logical representation in order to justify those inferences which on the basis of pre-logical intuitions we accept as valid. Logical representation is not a means of specifying the meaning of an isolated sentence, but instead a device for evaluating a specific inference in which the sentence may occur.

Logical analysis has thus its principal application to a special use of language, that of deductively inferring conclusions from premises. It can also be extended to assist in the solution of *specific* philosophical problems, and has proved successful as a means of criticizing mistaken inferences from grammatical form to ontological conclusions. The symbolism of logic is also useful as an abbreviating device for stating general conclusions not restricted to this or that particular example. But as a general theory of language and meaning it has not had and cannot have the success its advocates have hoped for it.

1.2 Ordinary language description

The so-called 'ordinary language' school of philosophy instituted by the later Wittgenstein, Austin, Ryle, and Strawson used a very different method. Instead of paraphrasing and representing sentences in the manner required for inference evaluation, they undertook to describe the use of a variety of categories of sentences, including imperatives, expressions of feelings and emotions, and reports of sensations, in addition to the fact-stating indicative sentences that occur in standard deductive inferences. There are rules governing the use of sentences in these various categories, and it becomes the role of philosophy to make them explicit. Of special interest are what Austin terms 'performatives,' sentences containing prefixes such as 'I promise that . . .' or 'I state that . . .' which are used by speakers to perform the speech acts described by their main verbs, verbs such as 'promise' or 'state'. But the explication of rules of use is also extended to sentences containing words such as 'believe', 'certain', 'voluntary', 'ought', etc., often with the intent of criticizing a traditional philosophic theory which is claimed to be based on a misunderstanding of their use.

Doubts must be raised about the long-term viability of this method. First of all, granted its success as a means of criticizing assumptions made in modern philosophy since Descartes, once the criticisms have been completed there seems little else to accomplish. There is a limited number of errors that can be presumed to have been made in the historical tradition because of a misunderstanding of key words of ordinary language. Having exposed them, at least this reason for studying the rules governing the use of ordinary language will come to an end. Indeed, this prospect is envisaged by Wittgenstein when he predicts the demise of philosophy once the 'therapy' of disclosing its violation of rules of ordinary language has been completed.

As for the constructive task of simply describing linguistic rules, this also threatens to come to an end as a distinctively philosophical project. The science of linguistics has gradually incorporated most of philosophy's main findings as it has extended beyond the study of the syntax of language to the fields of semantics and pragmatics. The rules governing the use of performatives and the presuppositions for this use, for example, have become the subject matter of pragmatics as a branch of linguistics, and the statement of these rules is virtually indistinguishable from that given by the ordinary language philosophers. Just as the *a priori* introspective psychology of modern philosophy was, in Austin's words, 'kicked upstairs' to become part of empirical psychology, so philosophic conclusions reached about language have supplied the foundations for new areas of linguistics.

An attempt to distinguish the philosophy of language from linguistics can be made by claiming that philosophy attempts to state *necessary* or essential features of language, features which every natural language *must* have, while linguistics states *contingent* features which languages *happen* to have as the result of the special needs and arbitrary choices of the communities in which they have evolved. Thus, it can be claimed, and with justification as we shall see in Chapter 5, that every sentence must have a subject-predicate structure, while the specific grammatical rules which specify agreement between nouns and verbs will vary from one language to another. These rules will then be the subject matter of linguistics, while the subject-predicate distinction is a philosophical one.[5] But linguistics is also concerned with specifying universal features of languages, features which are in fact shared by all the world's surveyable languages. Included among these are the subject-predicate structure of sentences, as well as universal phonological laws which place constraints on the permissible sequences of speech sounds, for all languages. These universal features are inferred on the basis of an inductive inference from empirical evidence, and are in this sense contingent features. How do we distinguish them from the necessary features sought by philosophy? Within the framework of language itself it is difficult to make this all-important distinction, and vague intuitions seem to become the final court of appeal.[6]

In fact, few philosophers in the ordinary language tradition (Strawson is a notable exception) have even attempted to confront this problem. Its critics have noted the almost indefinite variety of linguistic forms studied and the haphazard selection from among them that has often been made.[7] Often selected for attention, as we have noted, has been a word or phrase which is the source of what is claimed to be a confusion made by the historical tradition. But relevant though they may be for historical corrections, such selections seem to be totally irrelevant to a general theory of language. Again, certain features of language are presumably central for any such philosophic theory, but ordinary language descriptions do not themselves provide a basis for selecting some instead of others.

1.3 The role of semiotic

Semiotic attempts to remedy this defect by singling out for attention features of language which are both invariant for signs of different levels of complexity and which distinguish sentences as linguistic signs from more primitive signs. Instead of what can be termed *horizontal* classifications of linguistic forms within natural languages or within special language frameworks such as those of science, law, or art, semiotic attempts to develop *vertical* classifications for signs at different levels of complexity, including environmental natural events as objects of interpretation, signals without grammatical structure, and finally sentences as the basic elements of human communication. Necessary features of language then become those which are invariant at all levels of signs and which distinguish linguistic signs as a category fulfilling certain functions from those at lower levels. The subject-predicate structure of a sentence is more than a feature which happens to be shared by known natural languages; it is a feature that must appear at the linguistic level if the sign is to function there in a way different from what is characteristic at the levels of signals and natural events.

The starting point for semiotic is the same as for contemporary philosophy of language: the use of ordinary language. As language users this is what we are most directly aware of as constituting in Peirce's words the 'warp and woof' of human thought. Unique to semiotic is its attempt to extend analogically features initially arrived at by examining language use to more primitive signs, with logical features of language becoming the archetype on which analysis of these latter signs is developed.[8] By characterizing a sign X_1 as 'more primitive' than another X_2 I mean that the interpretation of X_1 lacks one or more features present in the interpretation of X_2, while features of X_1's interpretation are preserved in X_2's. Thus, a signal such as a warning cry is more primitive than a linguistic sentence, in so far as it lacks an internal subject-predicate structure which enables reference to distant objects. On the other hand, devices used to secure reference for signals are present in the use of sentences. A natural sign such as an odor interpreted by a deer as the sign of a predator is, in turn, more primitive than a signal in not being produced with a communicative intent that must be recognized in order to interpret the sign. But a signal can direct its interpreter's attention to a referent occasion in a way similar to that for natural signs. After describing the interpretation of more primitive signs on the basis of analogically extended features we can then determine more exactly which features of language use are in fact necessary. There is nothing at all circular in this procedure. We proceed from a rough characterization of language use to a more exact understanding of it later based on comparisons made to signs at lower levels. In this way terms such as 'sign', 'sign type', 'interpretation', 'significance', and 'reference' take on a generality of application beyond the starting point from which they are initially derived.

The procedure may be compared to that used by neurophysiologists in unlocking the mysteries of the human brain. Because of its overwhelming complexity neurophysiologists first study the far simpler structures of lower organisms, starting with the flat worm and proceeding on through the phylogenetic scale of reptiles, birds, and mammals. With this as a background the functioning of the parts of the human brain becomes more clearly understood. So too for language. As the product of a long evolutionary history it also displays bewildering complexity. The key to understanding its central features is to trace their development from more primitive signs, signs whose use and interpretation we can recover with some difficulty from our own experience, but which we can speculate as occupying the central part of the experiencing of the lower forms of life from which we have evolved.[9]

Philosophers of language have in fact selected out for their chief attention those features of language which allow extended application to primitive signs. Out of the great variety of possible inferences philosopher-logicians, at least in the early development of modern logic, selected out those whose representation exhibited the same fundamental features of sentence form that comparisons made by semiotic reveal. Similarly, not all features of ordinary language have been the objects of philosophical descriptions, and in this respect they differ from those found in the writings of linguists. Major consideration has in fact often been given to those features uniquely characteristic of linguistic signs or shared in common by signs at more primitive levels. But rarely have the reasons for the choice of these features been made explicit.

Paralleling the relation of the philosophy of language to linguistics are relations of semiotic to a host of empirical sciences, including ethological studies of animal communication systems, comparative psychology, psycholinguistics, kinesics, and paralinguistics. Philosophical semiotic is not a competitor with these empirical disciplines, since it is concerned with invariant and contrasting logical features of the special types of signs which each singles out for special study. But as we shall see, these sciences do provide the materials for the comparisons that semiotic seeks to make, and key discoveries within them inevitably have an important effect. Advances within these sciences force present-day semiotic to be a very different discipline from what it was for Peirce in the nineteenth century.

We can speculate that semiotic may also have a positive influence on the development of new sciences. Given the basic methodology of the biological sciences to seek descriptions of the more complex in terms of the relatively simple, it is surprising to find the contemporary discipline labelled 'cognitive psychology' or 'cognitive science' attempting to construct models describing the computational processes of the human brain which ignore comparisons to information processing in lower organisms. The causes of behavior for cognitive scientists are 'mental representations' as states of the brain, with these representations (or signs) identified with encoded sentence tokens.[10] Thus, the task of explaining a person bringing his umbrella in terms of his belief that it will rain and his desire to stay dry becomes reformulated as the task of explaining how the behavioral response of umbrella carrying is caused by the brain state encoding a token of the sentence 'It will rain' and an encoded token of 'I shall stay dry'. But obviously, it will be difficult to explain the operations of a system as complex as the human brain. Far more tractable would seem to be the problem of explaining the causal relation between the encoded internal signs of lower organisms and behavior as their effects.

The restriction of cognitive science to models postulating sentence tokens as the processed elements has led Paul Churchland to reject this entire approach as a means of explaining behavior in terms of psychological states. Infants prior to language acquisition and other infra-linguistic organisms, he argues, certainly are not processors of encoded sentence tokens. Yet how their wants and expectations affect their behavior and how they learn from experience seem continuous with how behavior is affected and learning accomplished for adult human language users. Hence, Churchland concludes that any model requiring processing of encoded sentence tokens cannot be adequate to the essential features of human cognition.[11] At least the beginning of a remedy may be provided by semiotic with its investigations of logical functions of signs interpreted by infra-linguistic organisms and their similarities and differences with the functioning of sentences as used by adult humans. An understanding of such functions may suggest some day ways of constructing empirically testable models which can successfully explain the continuities that Churchland is correct in emphasizing.

Semiotic as a sub-discipline in philosophy has been in existence since at least the early Middle Ages. Why has it been virtually ignored by the two main schools of the philosophy of language in this century? Why has language been analyzed and described in isolation from comparisons to non-linguistic signs? To answer these questions we must first review in the next chapter the history of the subject, paying special attention to difficulties which were later to block its progress and prevent it from assuming the role in the study of language which it should now be occupying. After this we can proceed to the constructive task of outlining the main similarities and differences between sentences and more primitive signs.

2 HISTORY OF SEMIOTIC

This chapter is devoted to providing the background essential for the systematic account of different levels of signs that begins with the next. I am not concerned here with providing a sequel to the excellent historical studies available in the recent literature. It is sufficient for our purposes to show the origins of some issues that will concern us later and to outline the main sides in the controversies arising from earlier solutions to basic problems. The most important of these involves the status of natural signs, signs not produced for the purposes of communication, and the relationship of these signs to linguistic signs. In the process of conducting this brief survey we will see how the conception of a sign has evolved through a long history of philosophical discussions. This presents us with the problem of selecting among alternative conceptions in defining the scope of semiotic in the final section of this chapter.

2.1 The Classical tradition

The Greek word for sign was '*to semeion*' (plural, '*ta semeia*'). The modern 'semiotic' is derived by way of a Medieval intermediary from the Greek *semeiotikos*, meaning an observant of signs, one who interprets or divines their meaning. From the earliest writings available to us, beginning with Hippocrates and Parmenides in the fifth century BC through to the discussions of such Roman writers as Cicero and Quintillian, writers in the classical period used the term '*semeion*' as a synonym for '*tekmerion*' to mean evidence, proof, or symptom of what was at least temporarily absent or hidden from view.[1] Examples commonly given were smoke as a sign of fire, clouds as a sign of an impending storm for the sailor at sea, and a flushed complexion as a sign for the physician of a fever. In all such examples we have one natural object or event which can be directly observed in the present standing for another which cannot be, though sometimes (rarely in philosophic discussions) '*semeion*' was also used in the sense of a sign or omen of the supernatural. It was also used to stand for facial expressions or behavior as signs of mental states themselves inaccessible to the observer, as blushing is a sign of shame or a grimace a sign of felt pain.

But the paradigm sign in the most extensive discussions available to us, those found in the writings of Sextus Empiricus,[2] was the medical symptom as a means of diagnosing the condition of a patient. The principal *semeiotikos* for classical philosophers was thus the physician seeking to determine a hidden disease in order to apply a cure. For Hippocrates, diagnosis involved discovering signs signifying the past and future as well as the present:

I hold that it is an excellent thing for a physician to practice forecasting. For if he discover and declare unaided by the side of his patients the present, the past, and the future, and fill in the gaps in the account given by the sick, he will be more believed to understand the cases, so that they will confidently entrust themselves to him for treatment.[3]

Quintillian was later to explicitly point out the three temporal directions of signs. He notes that a woman giving birth is a sign of past sexual intercourse, with the inference from sign to what is signified going from effect to prior cause, while a serious wound is the sign of death, with the inference now from a presently observed cause to a future effect.[4] In contrast, waves are a sign of contemporaneous wind, just as smoke is contemporaneous with fire, flushed complexion with a fever, etc.

Classical authors also distinguished, following Aristotle, infallible or necessary signs from 'refutable' or probabilistic signs which do not guarantee the presence of what they signify. As examples of necessary signs Aristotle gives a woman's giving milk as a sign that she lately bore a child and a fever as a sign of illness. Probabilistic signs are illustrated by fast breathing as a sign of fever, 'since a man may breathe hard without having a fever.'[5] The context of this distinction by Aristotle is a discussion of the rhetorical syllogism in his *Rhetoric*, a context which had, as we shall see, an important influence on the conception of signs later developed by the Stoics.

The most important controversy developed in these early discussions was that between the Stoics and the Epicureans, and centered on the status of the sign itself. As reported by Sextus Empiricus, the Stoics held that the term *'semeion'* stands for a proposition or 'intelligible' (*lekton*) describing an observable fact. As such it is a constituent of an inference in which we infer what the sign signifies or stands for. The form of this inference is *modus ponens*, with the sign as one premiss and the antecedent of the conditional or hypothetical which constitutes the other premiss. What the sign signifies is then inferred by detaching the consequent. In Sextus's words, for the Stoics, 'the Sign is an antecedent proposition in a valid hypothetical major premiss, which serves to reveal the consequent.'[6] The example of a hypothetical premiss given is 'If this man has had a viscid bronchial discharge, he has a wound in his lungs'. Having a bronchial discharge is a sign of the lung wound.

> For this premiss is valid, as it begins with the truth 'This man has had a viscid bronchial discharge', and ends in the truth 'he has a wound in his lungs'; and besides, the first serves to reveal the second; for by observing the former we come to an apprehension of the latter.[7]

More generally, if X is the sign and Y what it signifies, we can infer from X to Y by way of the inference.

$$\frac{X}{\text{If } X \text{ then } Y}$$
$$Y$$

In opposition to this inferential theory of the Stoics, the Epicureans are reported by Sextus to have held that the sign is a sensible particular, an object of direct observation rather than a proposition expressed within an inference. It is the observed smoke that is the sign of fire, not the proposition expressed by the sentence 'There is smoke over there'. First, they contended that the sign must be what signifies, and while utterances or written inscriptions signify propositions, propositions as intellectual conceptions do not themselves signify. Hence, 'as propositions are signified, but not signifying, the sign will not be a proposition.'[8] Second, they argued that illiterates and lower animals seem to be incapable of reasoning by *modus ponens*, but are capable of interpreting signs:

> . . . if the sign is a judgment [or proposition] and an antecedent in a valid major premiss those who have no conception at all of a judgment, and have made no study of logical technicalities, ought to have been wholly incapable of interpreting signs. But this is not the case; for often illiterate pilots, and farmers unskilled in logical theorems interpret by signs excellently. . . . Yet why do we talk of men, when some of the Stoics have endowed even irrational animals with understanding of the sign? For, in fact, the dog, when he tracks a beast by footprints, is interpreting by signs; but he does not therefore derive an impression of the judgment 'if this is a footprint, a beast is here'. The horse, too, at the prod of a goad or the crack of a whip leaps forward and starts to run, but he does not frame a judgment logically in a premiss such as this – 'If a whip has cracked, I must run'. Therefore the sign is not a judgment, which is the antecedent in a valid major premiss.[9]

The Epicurean view, as we shall see in the next chapter, is the superior for framing a general theory of signs inclusive of language, and we must recognize the soundness of both arguments. But it is important to notice how the choice of examples of signs selected by classical writers and the use of the medical symptom as the paradigm sign virtually dictated the Stoic view. In fact, it is by way of an inference capable of linguistic formulation that we infer from evidence such as smoke, a fever, a bronchial discharge, or a scar, to their past or present causes or future effects. Moreover, this is an inference that those unschooled in logic can make as easily as the educated. It does not, after all, require an ability to formulate the rule of *modus ponens* in order to use the rule for evidential reasoning, and in this sense the illiterate pilot or farmer is the equal of us all. If the examples of signs interpreted by animals had been used by the Stoics generally, then indeed they would have been guilty of the inconsistency being charged. But it is only 'some of the Stoics' who used these examples. More typical were examples given of signs which could only be interpreted by humans with their capacity to use language and draw inferences, and for these the inference from sign to what it signifies does conform to the Stoic pattern. For such objects or events – and they include all the so-called 'natural signs' of the Medieval tradition to follow – no significant analogy exists to the linguistic signs used in human communication. Instead, they are a constituent part of the use and interpretation of language at the sophisticated level of inferential reasoning.

This relationship between signs conceived by classical philosophers and inferential reasoning is illustrated by Sextus's criticisms of the Stoics' conception of what they called 'indicative' signs, signs which stand for what is unobservable, as sweating can be interpreted as a sign of invisible pores in the skin or behavior a sign of motions in the soul. These were contrasted with what were called 'associative' (or 'commemorative') signs. These latter are signs which stand for what is observable and for which there is a correlation in past experience between the sign and what it signifies, as illustrated by the observed correlation between smoke and fire, a scar and the wound that caused it, and a puncture of the heart and impending death. It is only the associative in Sextus's view that should be included as signs. He argues that a sign should be capable of being interpreted in a uniform way by all that observe it, but the indicative signs of the Stoics are interpreted in many different ways, with many different hidden causes assigned by physicians to symptoms where no observable correlation exists: 'The symptoms of fever, the flush, the moisture of the skin, the high temperature, the rapid pulse, when observed by doctors of the like constitution, are not interpreted in the same way.'[10]

This controversy between the Stoics and Skeptics can be seen to involve contrasting views of scientific causal explanation, with the sign playing the role of the explanandum (thing to be explained) and what it signifies stated as a premiss in the explanation. Sextus admits only generalizations established by induction from observations as premisses of an explanation. The presence of smoke can be explained by fire because we have observed a past correlation between the two. The Stoics, on the other hand, were willing to admit also theoretical explanations of events in which unobservables were posited. To explain sweating is to posit invisible pores in the skin, and in this sense the sweating is a sign of the pores. Again, the nature of examples appealed to, and especially the use of the medical symptom as the paradigm, requires sign interpretation to be understood as the use of an inference in which the sign is now reported in the conclusion. The question whether *Y* is what is signified by sign *X* becomes the question whether *Y* can be used to explain *X* as the premiss of an inference.

In none of these early discussions by classical philosophers do we find attempts to include within the extension of the term '*semeion*' words or sentences as linguistic signs. In the fragmentary writings of Parmenides there even seems to be a contrast drawn between signs (*semeia*) as reliable indicators of what they stand for and words (*onoma*) which are arbitrarily posited names introducing distinctions where none exist in the objective world. Thus, we have signs 'that Being is ungenerated and imperishable, whole, unique, immovable, and complete,' while the mistaken belief that 'things were born and now are, and from now on they will grow and will afterwards perish', arises from the act of introducing names for these things.[11] Sextus reports that the Stoics did include within the scope of their discussion certain conventional signs such as a torch signifying an approaching enemy or a bell signifying the selling of meat. These signs are 'determined, as they say, by the lawgivers and are in our power, whether we wish them to make known one thing or to be significative of many.'[12] But while they are used for purposes of communication, they are not signs formed within a rule-governed language, and do not present exceptions to the general exclusion of the linguistic. It is a short step to move from signs such as the torch and bell to linguistic signs, but it is one taken only later by St Augustine and the Medieval logical tradition that followed him.

Another apparent exception to this exclusion of the linguistic is presented in the opening passage of Aristotle's *De Interpretatione*, a passage destined to have an important influence on later discussions:

Spoken expressions are symbols [*symbola*] of mental impressions, and written expressions [are symbols] of spoken expressions. And just as not all men have the same writing, so

not all make the same vocal sounds, but the things of which
[all] these are primarily the signs [*semeia*] are the mental
impressions for all men. . . .[13]

This seems to state that verbal utterances are to be included
within the class of signs, along with natural events such as clouds,
smoke, and scars. Recall that behavior and facial expressions
were regarded as signs of mental states, as laughter is a sign of
joy. It seems to be a natural extension also to include a scream as
a sign of experienced fear, and finally a verbal utterance of 'I am
afraid' as a sign of this fear, as evidence from which we can infer
an emotion which itself we do not directly observe. Finally,
utterances of indicative sentences such as 'It is raining' can be
regarded as a basis for inferring the speaker's belief and
utterances of 'Close the door' for inferring his desire for the door
to be closed. By using *semeia* interchangeably with *symbola* for
spoken and written words as signs of the mental, Aristotle
himself strongly suggests this interpretation, for this is the same
term used in the *Rhetoric* to stand for necessary and probable
signs as evidence.

As Eco notes, however, Aristotle customarily refers to spoken
and written words, not as signs or *semeia*, as he does at the end
of the passage just quoted, but as symbols (*symbola*), arbitrarily
instituted marks with significance. Because they are arbitrary
they vary from one culture to another, and in this respect are
unlike spontaneous cries and most facial and behavioral expressions of emotions.[14] Moreover, the analogy Aristotle is
making in this *De Interpretatione* passage is that between the
relationship of written to spoken words on the one hand and
spoken words to mental experiences on the other. Now it is
incorrect to say that written words are evidence of the spoken.
Rather, we should say they replace spoken utterances, serving as
more permanent substitutes which enable communication at
greater distances, both spatially and temporally. If the analogy is
to hold, then spoken words are indicated in this passage also to
be a kind of replacement or substitute for the mental experiences, and not evidence for them. And just as the same spoken
words can be replaced by a variety of written marks, depending
on the culture's system of writing, so the same mental
experiences as shared in common by all can be replaced by a

variety of speech sounds. As we shall see in the next section, this is precisely the interpretation of this passage given by Ockham at the end of the Middle Ages.

For the classical period, then, the paradigm sign was a medical symptom, a natural occurrence serving as evidence for what it stands for. The sign could signify what is in the past, present, or future, and as a necessary sign could guarantee this other object or event or make it more or less probable as a 'refutable' sign. Spoken and written words were termed 'symbols' and contrasted with signs, though they were like signs if, as one possible interpretation of Aristotle suggests, they could function as evidence of the mental states of those producing them.

2.2 Augustine and his successors

During the Middle Ages a very different conception of the sign emerged. As represented by the Latin '*signum*' (plural, '*signa*') as the translation of '*semeion*', it now came to take on an extended generic sense that included both natural occurrences and linguistic expressions, distinguished now as 'natural' and 'conventional' signs. Increasing attention was focused on the latter, transforming the linguistic expression into the paradigm sign, and even by the time of Locke's *Essay*, leading to its supplanting the classical evidential sign as the paradigm sign.

The writer generally acknowledged as responsible for bringing about this fundamental change was St Augustine.[15] He accepts the Epicurean view of the sign as a sensed particular which signifies that which is not presently sensed: 'A sign is something which is itself sensed and which indicates to the mind some thing beyond the sign itself. [*Signum est quod et se ipsum sensui et praeter se aliquid animo ostendit.*]'[16] Under this very general heading are distinguished two kinds of signs. Natural signs [*signa naturalia*] are those which, 'without any intention or desire of signifying [*sine volantate atque ullo appetitu significandi*], make us aware of something beyond themselves, as smoke signifies fire.'[17] By using the Stoic example of smoke as a sign of fire Augustine demonstrates the link between his natural signs and the evidential signs of the Greeks. He seems to show no awareness, however, of the presence of linguistic mediation in the interpretation of such signs and the use of an inference noted by the Stoics.

Contrasted to natural signs were *signa data*, signs given or produced. Such signs are:

> those which living creatures show to one another for the purpose of conveying, in so far as they are able, the motions of their spirits or something which they have sensed or understood. Nor is there any reason for signifying, that is for giving signs, except for bringing forth and transferring to another mind what is conceived in the mind of the person who gives the sign.[18]

There is nothing in this characterization of *signa data* to warrant for them the customary label 'conventional signs.' The contrast to natural signs being drawn is between signs which are not intentionally produced for the purposes of communication and those that are. Signs produced with communicative intent, whether the intent is to express 'motions of spirits' or information about objects 'sensed or understood,' may not be conventional in the sense of conforming to a rule established within a linguistic community. A gesture made to communicate in a foreign country with someone not speaking one's language would seem to be a *signum datum* of the kind being defined here. But it may not be a conventional sign. Elsewhere Augustine characterizes the meaning of *signa data* as not given by nature, but arbitrarily stipulated and reached by consensus (*'non natura, sed placito et consensione significandi'*).[19] This does characterize so-called 'conventional signs,' but the addition is not necessary to distinguish a sub-class of signs distinct from natural signs. We shall see later in Chapter 4 the importance of distinguishing these two aspects of communicated signs.

Augustine is also responsible for a second innovation of fundamental importance. Recall Aristotle's analogy between the relation of written to spoken words and of spoken words to the mental states of the speaker. Augustine draws out this analogy to its logical conclusion. We must postulate, he concludes, 'mental words' as the mental correlates of spoken words, just as spoken words are the correlates of the written:

> The word heard sounding outside is the sign of the word which is luminous within, which is more appropriately called a 'word'. For what is brought forth by the mouth of the body is the

utterance of the word [*vox verbi*]; and though this, too, is called a 'word', it is so only on account of that which it is being used to manifest externally.[20]

The mental word or conception will be one which is common to all men, but for the purpose of 'transferring to another mind' the speaker must employ an arbitrarily selected conventional word unique to his linguistic community. If we identify these mental words with the mental states of the speaker, then it seems clear that spoken words will not signify or be evidence of these mental states. Rather, they will signify what the mental words do, that is, signify as equivalent public translations of private signs.

William of Ockham clearly draws this implication towards the end of the Middle Ages. Ockham pays lip service to the evidential sign of the Classical period, giving the traditional examples of smoke as a sign of fire, a groan the sign of pain, and laughter of a 'certain interior joy.' These are distinguished from words as conventional signs whose meaning is established by 'voluntary institution.'[21] But, like Augustine, Ockham's chief concern is with linguistic expressions and the relation between them and the thoughts or conceptions they express. This leads him to suggest a drastic revision of the natural–conventional sign distinction. It is now the mental conception itself which signifies naturally:

> The concept or the passion of the soul naturally signifies whatever it signifies [*naturaliter significat quidquid significat*]. The pronounced or written term, on the other hand, does not signify anything save by voluntary institution.[22]

Ockham explicitly rejects the view that the spoken word or term stands for or signifies the mental concept or 'passion of the soul.' Instead, it signifies those same independent objects which the concept or 'mental word' signifies.

> The conceived term is an intention, or passion of the soul, which by its nature signifies or cosignifies something. . . . These [mental] words remain in the mind only and cannot be brought to light externally, although words, as signs subordinated to them, are pronounced externally. . . . Words are used to signify those same things that are signified by the concept of the mind, in such a manner that first the concept signifies

something naturally and secondly the word signifies the same thing.[23]

For Ockham, then, there is a second type of natural sign, Augustine's mental word, and with attention focused increasingly on linguistic signs, the primary natural–conventional contrast was between mental words and the spoken and written words by which they are made public.[24]

The shift in focus towards the linguistic culminates in the restriction of the term 'sign' to linguistic expressions and their mental correlates in the writings of Hobbes and Locke. For Hobbes there are both private and public signs. Private signs are 'marks' (*notae*), that is, Augustine's mental words, which enable us to 'remember our own thoughts.' Public signs are 'signs by which we make our thoughts known to others.' 'The difference . . . betwixt marks and signs is this, that we make those for our own use, but these for the use of others.'[25] Both types of signs, public and private, are included in the scope of the branch of philosophy Locke later terms 'semiotic,' 'the business whereof is to consider the nature of signs, the mind makes use of for the understanding of things, or conveying its knowledge to others.'[26] Here the term 'sign' has virtually no recognizable affinity with the '*semeion*' of the classical period, which had excluded from the domain of signs exactly what it is now being restricted to.

There are uses of the term 'natural sign' in the period after Descartes in which the link to the early classical evidential signs is acknowledged, though in these the term is significantly modified and extended. Arnauld, for example, makes the traditional distinction between natural and conventional signs, but takes the former to stand in an iconic or picturing relation to what they signify, and distinguishes them by the presence or absence of a causal relation to their objects.

Signs may be divided into natural signs and conventional signs. Natural signs do not depend on the whim of man [*fantaisie des hommes*] – an image in a mirror is a natural sign of the person mirrored. A conventional sign is a sign established by convention and may, but need not, have any connection with the thing signified.[27]

The mirror image is the causal effect of the object mirrored or a process emanating from this object, just as smoke is the effect of fire and symptoms of some underlying disease. But unlike the classical evidential signs, we seem to infer from the mirror image to the object only in special circumstances, and Arnauld has thus introduced a novel category of natural sign. Maps and pictures are also listed by him as signs, but since they fail to stand in a causal relation to what they signify and depend on the 'whim of man,' they would seem to fall under the heading of his conventional signs, here widened also beyond Augustine's paradigm of the linguistic expression and the Stoics' torch and bell.

Still a further extension of the natural sign was made later when sensations themselves were regarded as natural signs of the objects producing them, thus combining Augustine and Ockham's mental aspect with Arnauld's iconic. This conception is perhaps most clearly stated by Reid in the eighteenth century. There are for Reid three categories of natural signs. The first includes the Stoic evidential signs, 'those whose connection with the things signified is established by nature, but discovered only by experience.'[28] But while the classical evidential sign was typically the effect of a cause, Reid regards interpretation as predictive: 'What we commonly call natural causes, might, with more propriety, be called *natural signs*, and what we call *effects*, the *things signified*.'

Reid's second category includes signs of human thoughts, purposes, and desires which are part of the 'natural language of mankind' prior to the institution of 'artificial language.'

> For all artificial languages presuppose some compact or agreement to affix a certain meaning to certain signs; . . . but there can be no compact or agreement without signs, nor without language; and therefore there must be a natural language before any artificial language can be invented.[29]

Signs within this 'natural language' are said to be 'modulations of the voice, gestures, and features.'

Finally, Reid adds as a third category of signs those whose signification is determined, not by prior experience of correlations, but by a kind of innate mechanism which suggests what is signified. These are signs which,

though we never before had any notion or conception of the
things signified, do suggest it, or conjure it up, as it were, by a
natural kind of magic, and at once give us a conception, and
create a belief in it.

Included in this third category are sensations as signs of external
objects, even though, like the Stoic indicative signs, the

connection between sensations and the conception and belief
of external existences, cannot be produced by habit, experience, education, or any principle of human nature that hath
been admitted by philosophers.

They are thus to be distinguished from signs of the first category.

The later controversy between realists and idealists then
became one regarding the status of natural signs. Realists
admitted signs of Reid's third category, though differed about
what they signified, with some (including Reid) holding that they
are signs only of the bare existence of objects, others that they
picture certain specific aspects of these objects. Idealists such as
Berkeley and perhaps Hume, on the other hand, admitted signs
only of the first category. They held that we do not perceive
objects, but only sensations, and a sensation such as that of the
sound of a coach is a sign of the coach only in the sense that in
prior experience the sound and the sight of the coach have been
correlated. Thus, in 'truth and strictness' for Berkeley, 'nothing
can be *heard* but *sound*; and the coach is not then properly
perceived by sense, but suggested from experience.'[30] Rather
than being signs of objects, sensations are signs of other
sensations with which they have been previously correlated.

By the beginning of the nineteenth century Augustine and his
modern successors had thus bequeathed a motley variety of
natural signs with differing relations to the so-called 'conventional' signs with which they were contrasted. Still retained were
the classical evidential signs, illustrated by the same examples as
those of the Greeks. But in addition there were also mental
conceptions or 'mental words,' mirror images as iconic signs, and
finally sensations as the 'internal' mental signs of the 'external'
objects that cause them. With Augustine spoken and written
words as the basic elements from which sentences are formed
became the paradigm signs. But as the variety of natural signs

increased, it became increasingly difficult to find common features that warranted applying the same term 'sign' to both these and the signs used in human communication.

2.3 Peirce and Saussure

The influences of these earlier views and many of their resulting confusions are evident in the writings of the philosopher generally credited to be the founder of modern semiotic. For Charles Peirce the term 'semiotic' is applied to what he calls the 'quasi-necessary, or formal, doctrine of signs.'

> By describing the doctrine as 'quasi-necessary,' or formal, I mean that we observe the characters of such signs as we know, and from such an observation, by a process which I will not object to naming Abstraction, we are led to statements, eminently fallible, and therefore in one sense by no means necessary, as to what *must be* the characters of all signs used by a 'scientific intelligence', that is to say, by an intelligence capable of learning by experience.[31]

The empirical studies by linguists of human language and ethologists of animal communication systems have as their aim the description of signs as actually used and interpreted. In Peirce's view semiotic as a branch of logic and philosophy has the same observational basis as do these related empirical sciences, but it aims at singling out necessary, as opposed to contingent, features of signs interpreted by creatures capable of learning. Just as a logical analysis of a sentence differs from a grammatical description that will vary from language to language, so too the semiotic description of a sign will differ from any empirical description.

It is obvious from this definition of semiotic that Peirce intended its scope to extend beyond the linguistic signs used in human communication. This is also shown by the generality of his definition of a sign or 'representamen' as 'something which stands to somebody for something in some respect or capacity.'[32] Under the heading of a sign as so defined Peirce includes single-word sentences such as 'Red' accompanied by a gesture, sentences with a subject-predicate structure, and even inferences consisting of several sentences, one of which, the conclusion, is inferred from the remaining as premisses. But also included are several kinds of non-linguistic signs. Among them under the heading of what he terms an 'index' are the examples of classical evidential signs where the sign is the causal effect of the object it is said to represent, e.g. the bullet hole as a sign of the bullet, the weathervane as a sign of wind direction, the falling barometer as a sign of coming rain. Also included under the heading of 'sign' are Arnauld's iconic signs which are related to their objects by similarity of structure, e.g. a painting, map, or diagram.

But though this very inclusive scope is intended by Peirce, his characterizations of signs seem often to show that the paradigm sign is in fact for him the sentence with subject–predicate structure. The sign, he tells us,

> can only represent the Object and tell about it. It cannot furnish acquaintance with or recognition of that Object; for that is what is meant . . . by the Object of a Sign; namely, that with which it presupposes an acquaintance in order to convey some further information concerning it.[33]

Neither a bullet hole nor a map would seem to represent in the way that is being described here, for they need not convey information about a particular object (a bullet or a town) with which the interpreter has some prior acquaintance. The bullet hole stands for some bullet or other, the dot on the map (without a name as label) for some indefinite town. In contrast, the predicate of a sentence such as 'John is tall' does convey information about an object with which the interpreter is assumed to have prior acquaintance; only with this can the referent of 'John' be identified. Thus, the passage seems directed towards the sentential paradigm, not towards signs in general.

This divergence between a general characterization extending to the traditional natural signs and one that is language-specific is reflected also in Peirce's treatment of two of his three major categories of signs, indices and symbols.[34] An index, he says, 'is a sign which refers to the Object that it denotes by virtue of being really affected by that Object.'[35] Besides bullet holes, weather-vanes, barometers, etc. Peirce includes under this heading photographs which, though they resemble their objects, and in this respect are like icons, have been 'produced under such circumstances that they were forced to correspond point by point to nature,' and are thus indices. An icon such as a diagram or map, in contrast, is produced in Arnauld's words by the 'whim of man.' Under this definition of an index its relation to its object is a dyadic causal one which would exist whether or not there were someone present to interpret it.[36] But Peirce also characterizes the index in a way that does necessarily involve an interpreter and that seems formulated with the sentence again in mind. 'Anything which focusses attention,' he says, is an index, and he gives as examples the demonstratives 'this' and 'that' as they occur in the subject position of a sentence. Such indices are not themselves the causal effect of objects, but devices which he says enable their interpreter to 'place himself in direct experiential or other connection with the thing meant.'[37]

A similar divergence of application arises in Peirce's treatment of a symbol. This is characterized as a sign which signifies by virtue of being an instance or token (or 'replica,' as he sometimes calls it) of a type (or 'legisign'). Thus, a verbal utterance or written inscription of the word 'red' signifies as a token of a type of expression. In this respect symbols differ from indices as particular effects of the objects they represent and icons as particular sensible images similar to their objects. This aspect of the symbol is captured in the following definition:

> A Symbol is a sign which refers to the Object that it denotes by virtue of a law, usually an association of general ideas, which operates to cause the Symbol to be interpreted as referring to that Object. It is thus itself a general type or law, that is, is a Legisign. As such it acts through a Replica.[38]

In this general sense of a sign which signifies by virtue of 'an association of general ideas,' the symbol would seem to have a scope far beyond linguistic signs, including, for example, even the flash of lightning which stands for thunder by virtue of associations in past experience. It would seem also to apply to the crack of a whip as a sign of running for the horse, the example used by the Epicureans in their rejection of the Stoic conception of the sign.[39] Both signify as tokens or replicas of general types of events as the result of prior learning, and are neither indices nor iconic representations. But Peirce also defines the symbol in a way more consistent with the traditional sense bestowed by Aristotle of a conventional sign whose meaning is determined by a linguistic rule: 'A Symbol is a Representamen whose Representative character consists precisely in its being a rule that will determine its Interpretant. All words, sentences, books, and other conventional signs are Symbols.'[40] As for the index and the sign in general, Peirce fails to adopt consistently a general definition which is then applied to the linguistic as a special case. Instead, he vacillates between an account applying only to linguistic signs and one with considerably wider scope.

Peirce has relatively little to say about the use of a sign by someone to communicate with another. It is perhaps for this reason that he fails to repeat Ockham's view that a spoken utterance or written inscription is a public manifestation of a private mental sign. But he does restate this doctrine in terms of the effect of a sign on one who interprets it. The 'logical interpretant' of a sign, he says, is the effect the sign produces in its interpreter, or its 'significate outcome.' This effect can be a thought, which he equates in common with Augustine and Ockham with a 'mental sign,' which represents the same object as does the original sign it translates. In this case it can also be interpreted and produce another mental sign, which in turn can be interpreted. But there is another type of effect that a sign can produce, and one that allows this process of sign translation to eventually terminate.

> Shall we say that this effect [produced by a sign] may be a
> thought, that is to say, a mental sign? No doubt, it may be so;
> only . . . it must itself have a logical interpretant; so that it
> cannot be the *ultimate* logical interpretant of the concept. . . .
> It can be proved that the only mental effect that can be so
> produced and that is not a sign but is of general application is a
> habit-change.[41]

This view that a habit is induced as the 'mental effect' of a sign, was destined to have, as we shall see in the next section, a decisive influence on behavioral formulations of semiotic that developed later.

After Peirce the study of signs took two very different directions, with the divisions marked largely along geographic lines. In Continental Europe the science of signs became known as 'semiology' and came to have an anthropocentric orientation. In the United States the key terms of semiotic were defined relative to the concepts of the emerging science of comparative animal psychology. The initial formulation of the program of semiology was provided by Ferdinand de Saussure. Semiology is to have as its subject matter, Saussure says, all the devices used in human society for the purposes of communication, including both linguistic expressions and non-linguistic devices such as gestures and signals within non-linguistic codes. Semiology in this conception is an empirical science, with linguistics a sub-division dealing with language as a special means of human communication:

> Language is a system of signs that express ideas, and is therefore comparable to a system of writing, the alphabet of deaf-mutes, symbolic rites, polite formulas, military signals, etc. But it is the most important of all these systems.
>
> *A science that studies the life of signs within society* is conceivable; it would be a part of social psychology and consequently of general psychology; I shall call it *semiology* (from the Greek *semeion* 'sign'). Semiology would show what constitutes signs, what laws govern them. . . . Linguistics is only a part of the general science of semiology; the laws discovered by semiology will be applicable to linguistics, and the latter will circumscribe a well-defined area within the mass of anthropological facts.[42]

Excluded by Saussure from semiology are the traditional natural signs and Peirce's indices, as well as signs used for communication by lower organisms. In another departure from Peirce's semiotic as a 'quasi-necessary' science studying features that must obtain of signs used by interpreters 'capable of learning by experience,' semiology restricts itself to features that in fact obtain of devices used in human communication. Logical analysis is thus abandoned in favor of empirical description characteristic of such sciences as sociology and anthropology.

Later European writers have accepted the main outlines of Saussure's program, with differences arising chiefly over its scope. All seem to agree in excluding natural signs. Guiraud, for example, excludes 'natural indications' such as clouds as signs of rain on the grounds that 'the cloud-laden sky has no intention of communication.'[43] There seems also to be general agreement that signs used for communication among lower animals should also be excluded, even though there may be reasons for believing they are used in some species of primates with communicative intent. Semiology is conceived as having an exclusively human orientation. Finally, there is agreement with Saussure that the methods of linguistics are to provide the model for studying non-linguistic modes of communication. In particular, the attempt is made to identify meaningful units analogous to the morphemes of human speech and rules analogous to linguistic syntactic and semantic rules by which such units are combined to form complex wholes.[44]

Not all writers have followed, however, the project of Roland Barthes and others to extend semiology to include complex cultural forms of communication, including film, theatre, music, dance, literature, architecture, advertising, and even food, clothing, and perfume by which persons indicate social status, sexual availability, etc. Such forms of expression have in Barthes's view a linguistic background constituted by areas which define the elements of the artistic or personal code being studied. It is 'the great signifying unities of discourse [*les grandes unités significantes du discours*]' providing this background that Barthes takes as the subject matter of semiology, and he claims it on these grounds to constitute a sub-division of linguistics.[45] The effect of making this extension to such a complex subject matter is to make it difficult to apply the methods of such sciences as linguistics, sociology, and anthropology, and this appears to threaten the goal of constructing a discipline in which consensus can be gained by co-operating investigators. Semiology becomes a vehicle for conveying personal interpretive insights rather than either Peirce's logical, philosophical study or the empirical science envisaged by Saussure.

2.4   Behavioral semiotic

A very different direction was taken by those writers who took as their project the extension of the methods of behavioral learning theory to the study of signs. In early formulations the paradigm sign became the conditioned stimulus of the conditioned reflex learning experiments, e.g. the bell paired with the unconditioned stimulus of food particles on a dog's tongue evoking the reflex response of salivation. The bell as an acoustic stimulus becomes a sign of the food as a tactual stimulus so far as it comes to evoke by itself at least a part of the response previously evoked only by the food. One of the earliest formulations of this approach was given by Ogden and Richards in their *The Meaning of Meaning*. It is a feature of the interpretation of a sign, they say,

> . . . that when a context has affected us in the past the recurrence of merely a part of the context will cause us to react in the way in which we reacted before. A sign is always a stimulus similar to some part of an original stimulus and sufficient to call up the engram formed by that stimulus.
>   An engram is the residual trace of an adaptation made by the organism to a stimulus.[46]

In the classical reflex learning experiments the paired bell and food constitute the whole 'context' and the bell on a given occasion is similar to some 'part' of this whole. As a sign the bell 'calls up' the response or 'residual trace of an adaptation' to the whole stimulus. The attempt is then made by these writers to extend this analysis of primitive signs to the interpretation of linguistic expressions.

Behavioral semiotic was an attempt to transform semiotic into an empirical science by proposing operational definitions of such traditional terms as 'meaning', 'denotation, and 'truth' which enable the process of sign interpretation to be investigated in terms of correlations between stimuli and responses as publicly observable events. Of these the term 'meaning' or 'significance' was of central interest, and became the focal point for the project of correcting what was regarded as the 'mentalistic' bias of traditional semiotic. In Ogden and Richard's version, what we shall refer to as the 'direct response theory,' the significance of a sign was explicated in terms of a given type of response to a type of stimulus. If we use XY for the entire context of which the sign X is one part and Y is the unconditioned stimulus evoking in isolation the response R the other, then Y can be said to be the significance of X for an interpreter I, according to this theory, if and only if X by itself evokes a response R' in I similar to or part of the R evoked by Y. Thus, the tactile stimulus of food particles on the dog's tongue is the significance of the bell for the dog in the classical experiments, since the bell in isolation evokes a salivation response similar to that evoked by the food.

The direct response theory then attempts an extension of this analysis to the significance of sentences for language users. Suppose that the visual stimulus correlated to an apple evokes a salivation response in a person. Then if the single-word sentence 'Apple' evokes a similar response, this visual stimulus is now regarded as the significance or meaning of the sentence.[47] In this form the theory seems to be implausible, since for few of the sentences a person hears and understands are there the overt responses R' it requires. It is highly unlikely that for a given person hearing 'Apple' there will be a detectable salivation response. Later versions of the direct response theory, the most influential of which is that formulated by C.E. Osgood, attempted to remedy this difficulty. For Osgood the responses evoked by signs are internal 'representational mediational responses,' neurophysiological in nature and detectable therefore only by special forms of observation. If a sign X causes an internal process R' in a subject I which is similar to a process R caused by a type of stimulus Y with which it has been paired, then Y can be said to be the significance of X for I.[48] But as critics of this version have noted,[49] there are formidable difficulties it must also face. First of all, there seems to be no experimental evidence that sentences as linguistic signs cause internal processes similar to those caused by the stimuli with which they are correlated in language learning, and the 'mediational' processes seem thus to be simply postulated as devices for saving the theory. Second, and more important, there seems to be no criterion for deciding whether one internal process is similar to another in the way required by the theory. Everything is similar in *some* respect to every other. Without a specification of that respect in which process R' is to be claimed as similar to R it would seem to be impossible to establish empirically the significance of a sign X. Yet it is precisely this sort of empirical determination that is the avowed central goal of behavioral semiotic.

As an alternative to defining significance in terms of a direct response to the sign itself, several philosophers have proposed an alternative that we shall refer to as the 'dispositional theory.' According to it a sign's significance is to be determined by a disposition of its interpreter to respond in certain ways to some subsequent stimulus. In its original formulation by Charles Morris the sign is defined as a 'preparatory stimulus' whose significance is a type of stimulus *Y* if it causes a disposition in its interpreter to respond in a way similar to that with which it responds to *Y* in isolation.[50] The disposition that is induced can be regarded as Peirce's habit change as the sign's 'logical interpretant.' Thus, a buzzer is a sign of food for a dog if it causes the dog to search for food and if on finding it at a given location the dog eats the food. The properties of the food evoking this subsequent eating response are regarded as the buzzer's significance.[51] This account is fraught with difficulties, as the responses that Morris requires include those to the sign itself (searching for food) and a subsequent stimulus (the visual stimulus of the food). The complexity of this response, the differing ways it can be interpreted, and again the problem of establishing criteria for similarity of responses – all of these factors ensure that this formulation can never be fruitful as a basis for experimental studies of the process of sign interpretation.

Later formulations of the dispositional theory by Carnap[52] and Quine[53] directed towards language interpretation, however, offer more promise. In them the significance of a sentence for a person is defined in terms of the disposition of that person to respond when queried by either 'Yes' or 'No' when presented with a given type of object. The subsequent response is in this manner simplified as one of two readily identifiable alternatives. Quine states his version in terms of the problem of determining the meaning of expressions in an alien language. Suppose a linguist were confronted with the problem of determining the meaning of a single-word sentence such as 'Gavagai' and had access to a native speaker. Then, by successively pointing to different kinds of objects and asking 'Gavagai?' the linguist should be able to solve his or her problem by noting those objects which evoked an affirmative response from the native (e.g. a nod of the head) and those which elicited a negative response. The 'affirmative stimulus meaning' of the single-word sentence 'Gavagai', Quine says, is simply that type of visual stimulus that evokes an affirmative response, while the 'negative stimulus meaning' is that which evokes a negative response. If on varying the objects and their properties and noticing that the informant consistently responds affirmatively to rabbits and negatively to other objects, the linguist can hypostatize that 'Gavagai' in the native language is synonymous with 'Rabbit' in English.

Difficulties confront this theory as a successor to either the direct response theory or Morris's alternative. One is that it will be difficult to identify a given gesture as an affirmative or negative response; such gestures are conventional ones which can vary markedly from one culture to another. Another difficulty is that the affirmative and negative responses by informants are voluntary responses that can be withheld. Informants certainly have the *capacity* to distinguish between objects to which an expression applies and those to which it does not, but whether this can be termed a disposition to respond to given types of stimuli is questionable. Certainly the term 'disposition' is being applied in a way different from that in which it is applied to the elasticity of rubber, the brittleness of glass, etc., and this difference is left unexplained. Some may want to interpret 'disposition' as synonymous with 'tendency', and claim that it only implies a probability that a response will be elicited by a given stimulus. But this then leaves it totally mysterious as to why the response is forthcoming on some occasions, while absent on others. Quine's theory differs from his predecessors' in being restricted to language interpretation. After the dog hears the buzzer there may be a detectable affirmative response when it later sees the food (e.g. muscular relaxation or an identifiable neurological process) and a negative resonse (e.g. muscular tension) when the food is absent at a given location. If so, the significance of the buzzer for the dog could conceivably be defined in terms of the types of visual stimuli that evoke these responses. But the task of identifying both the stimuli and the affirmative and negative responses is a formidable one, and at present there is only a hope that it could be solved.[54]

More fundamental objections to the dispositional theory have been raised by Chisholm, and are directed towards what appear to be irreducibly intentional aspects of sign interpretation.[55] Consider a native informant of whom the linguist asks the question 'Gavagai?' and points to a brownish, furry object that is not a rabbit but instead a squirrel. The informant, however, mistakenly believes it is a rabbit and hence responds in the affirmative. From the native's response the linguist cannot infer that the visual stimulus from the squirrel is the affirmative meaning of 'Gavagai' or that the word is synonymous with the English 'Squirrel'. Hence, the possibility of error seems to rule out the dispositional theory. Of course, normally the informant is correct, and after several repetitions the linguist should be able to translate the word correctly. But then we must revise our statement of the theory and say that the language disposition being characterized is only a tendency for assent or denial relative to types of stimuli. As before, there is the problem of explaining divergences of response. Negation poses a parallel problem. The negative stimulus meaning of a sign is for Quine constituted by those stimuli which evoke a negative response. But it seems possible for the linguist to point to a blank space with only background 'noise' impinging on the native's sense receptors. Here it is the *absence* of any stimuli which would evoke the negative response, not some stimulus other than that correlated with rabbits. The native has the capacity to recognize the absence of a rabbit at the location pointed to, but this capacity cannot be explicated in terms of a disposition to respond to a specific type of stimulus.

So far we have been discussing signs conveying information. For signs prescribing actions, e.g. the Epicurean example of the crack of the whip as a sign of running for the horse or the verbal commands 'Run' or 'Go', a version of the direct response theory would seem applicable, and the significance of the sign defined as the response it elicits as its effect.[56] But the obvious objection to this theory is that a person may disobey a given command, and even the horse may not run at the sound of the whip. The sign may have a certain action as its significance, though no response is observed. Again, for such a sign to have significance for an interpreter I there must be a capacity on I's part to recognize what action constitutes obedience to it.

The behavioral theories considered above have all been attempts to formulate empirical tests for determining the significance of a sign for an interpreter. B.F. Skinner has developed a version of behaviorism directed towards the production of signs by a communicator. The model for him is provided by instrumental learning, learning in which an organism's response to a given stimulus are determined by a schedule of positive or negative reinforcements. One standard experimental situation is that in which an animal learns to press a bar on seeing a flash of light if the pressing is positively reinforced by the reward of a food pellet. The light is the 'controlling stimulus,' while the learned response to this stimulus is the 'operant.' The animal learns to discriminate that controlling stimulus (e.g. the color of the light), which, when followed by a given operant, is reinforced from other stimuli for which reinforcement is absent. Skinner then extends the analysis of this primitive model to language learning. For descriptive words (e.g. 'red' or 'book'), or what he terms 'tacts,' learning occurs when verbal responses as operants, that is, utterances of the word, are selectively reinforced in the presence of controlling stimuli. 'A child is taught the names of objects, colors, and so on when some generalized reinforcement . . . is made contingent upon a response which bears an appropriate relation to a current situation.'[57] For prescriptions or 'mands' (e.g. the commands 'Go!' and 'Run!'), learning takes places in the absence of a definite controlling stimulus, with reinforcements in the form of obeying the command shaping the child's verbal behaviour. Skinner's variant of behaviorism has had little direct influence on philosophic formulations of semiotic. It did inspire, however, an attack on the entire behavioral program for analyzing language learning that was to have considerable influence.

Behavioral theories, especially those of Morris and Skinner, have had an important role in establishing the conceptual framework for behavioral studies of animal communication by ethologists such as Tinbergen, Lorenz, and Thorpe. Sign use and interpretation in this domain is studied in what Sebeok terms 'zoosemiotics,' as contrasted to 'anthroposemiotics,' the study of signs used in human communication, an area including linguistics, paralinguistics, the study of non-verbal behavior accompanying language use (e.g. pointing gestures, voice pitch), and kinesics, the study of non-verbal behavior used independently to communicate (e.g. bodily movements, facial expressions).[58]

2.5   Semiotic's critics

From this brief historical survey we can distinguish three main versions of semiotic, with variants for two of them. The first is the Greek conception of it as the theory of evidential signs, with the paradigm being the medical symptom as evidence of a disease as its cause. This should be regarded only as a stage on the way to the conceptions that followed, and not having a major influence on recent discussions.[59] The second conception is that of Locke for whom, as we have seen, semiotic is the theory of language as the primary means of communication, a conception brought about by Augustine's shift to the word as the paradigm sign. As a variant of Locke's conception we have the extension of the term 'sign' by Saussure and his followers in the semiological tradition to non-verbal means of human communication and the forms of discourse they presuppose. And finally, we have Peirce's conception of semiotic as the study of necessary features of signs used by creatures capable of learning from experience, including signs used for the purposes of communication and natural events that are not. The precursor of this conception was the Medieval application of 'sign' to both 'natural' and 'conventional' signs. A variant of Peirce's conception is found in attempts to analyze sign interpretation and use in terms of the controlled learning situations with animal subjects studied by behavioral psychologists. Signs to which this behavioral variant can be extended include those used in animal communication, the subject of Sebeok's zoosemiotics.

We shall understand in this work the term 'semiotic' to stand for the discipline delimited by Peirce, with its subject including linguistic and non-linguistic signs, and including natural events not produced for the purposes of communication. We shall also follow Peirce in understanding the term to apply to the logical study of necessary features of signs as interpreted and used, thus distinguishing it from those related empirical sciences which describe contingent features which observed signs happen to have. By adopting Peirce's conception we distinguish semiotic both from what is known as the 'philosophy of language,' the modern term for Locke's semiotic, and from semiology. Any such selection from among alternatives is arbitrary, but at least ours can be justified by the continuous history of Peirce's inclusive conception from St Augustine until the present.

Why has this discipline received so little attention from English-speaking philosophers in recent years? Its neglect seems to have been based on several important methodological concerns which serve to throw into question the possibility of semiotic as a general theory of signs. The first of these is directed towards any generic definition of a sign that is constructed with sufficient generality to include linguistic and non-linguistic signs.

Recall Peirce's general definition of a sign as 'something which stands to somebody for something in some respect or capacity.' For a sign to stand for something or for it to mean something for an interpreter would seem for it to stand in a relationship that can vary markedly, depending on the type of sign being considered. Gilbert Harman states this objection as follows:

> Smoke means fire and the word 'combustion' means fire, but not in the same sense of 'means.' The word 'means' is ambiguous. To say that smoke means fire is to say that smoke is a symptom, sign, indication, or evidence of fire. To say that the word 'combustion' means fire is to say that people use the word to mean fire. Furthermore, there is no ordinary sense of the word 'mean' in which a picture of a man means a man or means that man. This suggests that Peirce's theory of signs would comprise at least three different subjects: a theory of the intended meaning, a theory of evidence, and a theory of pictorial description. There is no reason to think that these theories must contain common principles.[60]

If there are no common principles relating the smoke, the word 'combustion', and the picture of a man as signs, then semiotic as the theory of such principles would seem to be impossible. This same criticism can be directed towards Karl Buhler's definition of a sign as a 'representative' ('*Stellvertrendes*') which 'stands in for something or someone,' and is applied to linguistic expressions, an actor portraying a character in a play, a lawyer representing his client, and a canvas picturing a landscape.[61] It is again difficult to see how such diverse senses of 'standing in for something' can exhibit common features which constitute a domain for study.

This reasoning can be extended to attempts to frame a sign theory that includes language and animal communication systems. Chomsky has criticized such attempts for arriving at a level of generality which must include much that is non-communicative and bears no obvious analogy to language. Suppose we define a communicated sign as that which is purposive, exhibits organization of elements or a syntax, and is informative. Then, Chomksy argues, this definition can be applied to a behavioral activity such as walking, for it is purposive or goal-directed, and there is an ordering among the separate movements, the flexing of muscles, positioning of the heel, etc. It is also informative, for the rate at which a person walks can indicate to another how strong is his want for the goal towards which he is directed. But there is obviously no significant analogy between walking and a sentence used to communicate.[62]

The similarities between semiotic and that pseudo-science known as 'general systems theory' that enjoyed a brief vogue in the 1960s and 1970s, and the type of enthusiasm both have inspired, should serve as an ominous warning. The latter theory proposes a definition of what is called a 'system' that is general and indefinite enough to be applied to humans, lower animals, a lake (an 'ecosystem'), the solar system, atoms ('systems' with a nucleus and orbiting electrons), and even a galaxy. This variety and scope of applications may serve to evoke in its adherents attitudes of wonder and awe. But no common features seem to hold of the types of objects called 'systems' that have justified the establishment of a science with identifiable problems, nor has there been the development of a method for reaching that consensus on conclusions essential for progress in any discipline. In the same way nearly everything within a suitable context can be classified as a 'sign' if the term is defined with sufficient generality. But it is unlikely that this chaotic variety will be one for which significant problems are formulated and solved by means of an agreed upon method.

Another major reason for the rejection of semiotic is the belief that linguistic signs possess unique features that resist attempts at assimilation to signs of more primitive types. The most well-known statement of this view is provided by Chomsky's criticism of the analysis by Skinner of language acquisition in terms of instrument learning outlined at the end of the previous section. The extension of such terms derived from animal learning as 'controlling stimulus', 'operant response', and 'reinforcement' to language acquisition, Chomsky contends, is a 'metaphorical extension' or a series of 'analogic guesses' which only serve to obscure the important differences between the two types of learning. What is created is only the 'illusion of a rigorous scientific theory with very broad scope.'[63]

Also criticized have been the attempts of the semioticians to extend terms from their application to sentences to non-linguistic signs. Austin criticizes the extension of 'truth' to pictures and the classical natural sign, e.g. smoke as a sign of fire:

A picture, a copy, a replica, a photograph – these are *never* true in so far as they are reproductions, produced by natural or mechanical means: a reproduction can be accurate or life-like. . . , but not true (of) as a record of proceedings can be. In the same way a (natural) sign *of* something can be infallible or unreliable but only an (artificial) sign *for* something can be right or wrong.[64]

It is only an utterance or inscription of a sentence as a conventional sign which can be said to be 'true.' To extend the term beyond this application is again to ignore the unique features of language. This criticism can be extended to Morris's attempt to apply the term 'true' to a sign such as the buzzer interpreted by the dog. 'From the point of view of behavior,' says Morris, 'signs are "true" in so far as they correctly determine the expectations of their users.'[65] But for such signs, as for the picture or photograph, there are no rules governing their use, and hence conditions for applying such normative terms as 'true' or 'correct' seem to be absent. Just as suspect is Morris's application of the logical term 'denotation' to primitive natural signs.[66] The subject of a sentence such as 'John' in 'John is tall' can be used to refer to an object on a given occasion, but a natural sign with no internal structure such as the buzzer interpreted by the dog has, as we shall we see in the next chapter, very different features.

These are important criticisms which cannot be simply dismissed, and indeed are indicative of serious difficulties in early expositions. One of these arises from the controversy over the status of the sign between the Stoics and Epicureans noted in Section 2.1, with the Stoics holding that signs as evidence are premises of an inference. Another is suggested by the vacillation by Peirce between definitions for signs with potentially broad scope and those restricted to the sentential paradigm. Finally, through the influence of Morris semiotic has been identified by many with the behavioral variant of Peirce's conception of the subject. The difficulties of extending a terminology derived from experimental situations involving animal learning to human language use are thus regarded as fundamental to semiotic. To the extent that contemporary semiotic has perpetuated such difficulties its critics are on strong ground.

In the chapters that follow I attempt to provide two remedies to these difficulties. The first of these is to specify the differences as well as similarities between the various levels in a more careful way than has been done before. The alternative to a vacuous generic conception of a sign is to restrict ourselves to simply describing the features which hold of signs as interpreted natural events, primitive signs used in communication, and sentences as the complex signs used in communication, with the goal of isolating features which signs at these different levels must have. We impose no requirement from the beginning of our inquiry that such comparisons will lead to some feature or set of features shared by signs at all levels. The second remedy is to restrict the term 'sign' more narrowly than has been the practice, with only those objects of interpretation which bear important analogies to linguistic expressions included within its scope. As we shall see in the next chapter, this requires excluding the classical evidential signs, the 'natural signs' of the Medieval tradition, and also certain physical and mental images, e.g. photos, mirror images, and Reid's sensations as signs. It will also require, as we shall see in Chapter 4, that only a very selective sub-class of animal signals be listed as communicated signs.

Finally, I concede to semiotic's critics the inadequacy of behavioral formulations that extend analysis of animal learning to language use. There are important analogies between the capacity of a lower animal to associate an event in its environment with either another event or an action and the human capacity to interpret linguistic expressions. But given the complexity and variability of human behavior, behavioral reductionism has proven an unsuccessful method for specifying these analogies, and I make no attempt to provide still another version. A more fruitful method, as I hope to be able to show, starts with the logical analysis of necessary features of language and extends the results of this analysis to features of more primitive signs encountered in human experience by abstracting from language's special features. This analogical extension of logical features is designed to replace the vague metaphors derived from animal learning experiments of the kind criticized by Chomsky. All can agree that there is a neurophysiological basis to the capacity of all organisms, human and non-human, to interpret signs. But reductionist accounts of logical terms such as 'significance', 'denotation', and 'truth' will not advance our scientific understanding of the physical structures and processes that provide this basis. These terms have their own appropriate application to language use as described by those who are engaged in it. Their application to more primitive signs can only be derived on the basis of our understanding of this primary use by extending the standard logical analyses of language, not by inventing for the terms entirely new applications.

3 NATURAL SIGNS

We turn now to our central task, that of specifying the essential features of signs of differing levels of complexity. We begin with the simplest level, that of natural signs as objects or events in the environment of their interpreter which are not produced by some agent with the intent to communicate. Our historical sketch has shown a great variety of signs to have been classified under this heading, including the classical evidential signs, material images, and sensations. We now look more critically at these classifications with an eye towards developing a conception of a natural sign for which important analogies to linguistic signs hold. We thus consider evidential signs in the first section of this chapter and images, both material and sensory, in the second. In the final two sections are outlined the essential features of a severely restricted range of signs that we label 'natsigns' and distinguish from the natural signs of the tradition.

3.1 Signs and evidence

We have already discussed in Section 2.1 the basic features of the classical evidential signs. What is signified by such signs is thought to occur either in their past, be contemporaneous with them, or occur in their future. When it lies in the past the sign seems invariably to be regarded as an effect and what it signifies the sign's cause, as the scar is said to be a sign of the past wound that caused it. If we include such signs of what lies in the past under the heading of what Peirce terms an 'index', e.g. a fossil as a sign of past life, a bullet hole as a sign of a fired bullet, and boulders as a sign of past glacial activity,[1] then the cause can lie in the remote past of the sign which is its effect. Indeed, the temporal interval between them can span millions of years. Where the sign is contemporaneous with what it signifies the relation again is normally understood to be causal, though examples have been given where this is not the case. Certainly medical symptoms of a disease (e.g. fever and vomiting as symptoms of influenza, spots as a symptom of measles) and smoke signifying fire are causal effects of that which they signify. But Peirce also gives the example of man's rolling gait being a sign he is a sailor (see note 5 of 2.3) and classical writers spoke of flushing as a sign of shame or laughter as a sign of joy. For such examples the term 'sign' seems to be used in the sense of 'criterion for': the rolling gait constitutes at least part of the criteria we use in identifying an individual as a sailor; the blushing is part of the criteria used in describing a person as ashamed. Being a sailor does not cause the rolling gait, nor does shame as a mental state cause the blushing.[2]

Where what is signified is to occur in the future, again the relation is normally, but not necessarily, causal, with the sign now the cause and what it signifies or means its effect. As for signs of past events, the temporal interval between the two may be of a long duration. H.H. Price distinguishes between "short-range" natural signs where the interval is relatively short and there is direct association in prior experience and "long-range" signs where what is signified lies in the relatively remote future.[3] Lightning as signifying thunder is an example of the former, since thunder follows the flash of lightning in a matter of seconds. Another example would be Hume's sight of the flame as a sign of intense heat for the learning child. In contrast, clouds are a long-range sign of the rain to follow, as would be a crack in a building's foundation as a sign of its eventual collapse and the rate of a star's combustion a sign of its later explosion. Here the interval may be hours, years, or even millions of years, and no direct association in prior experience between the sign and what it stands for is required for interpreting the sign. For these long-range signs of what occurs in the future the relation between sign and signified is not necessarily causal. The metabolic rate of the potato usually rises about forty-eight hours before a fall in barometric pressure, and thus this rising rate can be interpreted as a sign of the falling pressure. But the former clearly cannot be said to be the cause of the latter.[4]

Besides distinguishing natural signs with respect to temporal direction the tradition has followed Aristotle in also distinguishing necessary from probable signs. Thus smoke could be said to be a necessary sign of fire, a striated rock a sign of past life, a red shift in a spectral line a necessary sign of a receding galaxy, etc. These signs are 'necessary' in the sense that their presence invariably assures the presence of what they signify. In contrast, spots are only a probable sign of measles and clouds a probable sign of rain. As examples of indices Peirce sometimes cites signs which only signify with a high degree of probability, as a low barometer with moist air is an index of rain, for 'we suppose that the forces of nature establish a probable connection between the low barometer with moist air and coming rain.'[5]

These distinctions and virtually all of the examples used to illustrate them indicate that what are called 'natural signs' in the tradition that begins with Augustine are not primitive signs to be contrasted or compared with linguistic signs. Instead, they are examples of evidence whose interpretation requires the use of a linguistic empirical generalization. This generalization is usually a causal generalization and the evidence either an instance of either the cause of effect described within it. The interpreter infers from the evidence to what it stands for by means of the generalization. Thus, to interpret on a given occasion clouds as evidence of rain requires first formulating or being aware of the causal generalization 'Clouds cause rain', or better, 'Clouds are a sufficient causal condition of rain.' From the clouds that are observed we infer by way of the generalization to the predicted rain. More generally, if evidence x is an instance of an event, state of affairs, or object[6] of type X and its effect is of type Y, then given that X is the sufficient cause of Y a person can infer from the presence of x to a later instance of Y. The form of inference used in making the prediction, is thus

X is the sufficient cause of Y
Evidence x occurs (is present)
_____
There will be (is) an occurence of Y

Upon observing the evidence x its interpreter infers to the conclusion by means of the first premiss. Where the relation is not causal, as for the metabolic rate of the potato and falling atmospheric pressure, the first premiss becomes a generalization of the form 'Whenever X occurs Y will also.' Where we can anticipate an occurrence of Y with only a certain degree of probability, the first premiss is of the form 'X is the probable sufficient cause of Y' or 'The probability of Y given X is r', where r is some rational number less than 1 but greater than zero (symbolically $p(Y/X) = 0 < r < 1$). From such a premiss and the observation of evidence x we infer to 'The probability of Y occurring is r'.

When the evidence stands for what is in the past or for what is contemporaneous with it the generalization required for its interpretation is a causal generalization stating that X is the necessary causal condition of Y or that if X were (or had been) absent then Y would not have occurred. On the basis of such a generalization we can infer from an instance y of evidence Y to a past or contemporaneous occurrence of X. Thus, we infer from the scar to the past wound as its necessary cause and from smoke to the present fire. The form of inference used is

X is the necessary cause of Y
Evidence y occurs (is present)

There has been (is) an occurrence of X

As before, the first premiss can be the statement that X is the probable necessary cause of Y or a statistical generalization of the form '$p(X/Y) = 0 < r < 1$'. We infer from the presence of spots to only the probability of measles, because the spots may occur even though the patient does not have the disease and the disease is not therefore the invariable cause of them.

In cases where what the evidence stands for is remote in time, e.g. past life for the fossils, glacial activity for the boulders, the star's explosion for its rate of combustion, the inference forms are obviously oversimplified. Here the causal generalization will be embedded in a complex structure of supplementing physical theories and background information. Barthes has argued that medical diagnosis of symptoms also requires a context of medical and clinical discourse, and hence the interpretation of a symptom is only possible *'par la médiation du langage.'*[7] Here also it will not be a single generalization but a complex of them that makes possible the inference from evidence. The simplified forms that have been presented seem typical only of inferences made in daily life outside the framework of the special sciences. What we can conclude, however, is that *all* interpretation of evidence requires the mediation of *at least one* empirical generalization, though several may be required and the inference from the evidence may involve complex calculations.

Readers will recognize this account of evidence interpretation to be essentially the same as the Stoic view summarized in 2.1, that what is called a 'sign' is a propositional constituent of an inference. Why accept it? Perhaps the best reason is that only a species capable of using language could interpret the examples of evidential signs given by the tradition. Certainly lower animals cannot interpret such signs, even of the relatively simple variety as clouds as a sign of rain. In arguing against Barthes's view that medical symptoms are interpreted only relative to linguistic discourse Sebeok claims that domestic animals can perceive and act upon symptoms exhibited by humans.[8] But reports of such behavior seem usually to be projections of human capacities on lower animals. In the movies the dog Lassie may search for aid on observing her master's broken leg, but responses to such injuries seem at best instinctive responses that seem to involve no prior inference to their causes. Most lower animals learn to interpret one event as a sign of another only where the sign and what it signifies are either contiguous or separated by a relatively short temporal interval, such as the dog learning to interpret the bell as a sign of food. Psychologists have observed that as the temporal interval extends beyond a brief duration (as measured in seconds), the capacity for sign interpretation disappears. It would then be impossible for these animals to extend interpretation beyond this interval, let alone to extend it to absent causes separated in time by hours, days, or years. Higher primates and perhaps some other mammals do exhibit what we can perhaps describe as 'long-range planning': the tiger waiting for his prey at the water hole or stalking him by following traces, the chimpanzee hiding food to be eaten at a later occasion, etc. For such cases we can speculate that perhaps some kind of non-linguistic mental schemas (possibly internal mental analogues of the signals to be discussed below in 4.3) serve to mediate between one perceived event and another anticipated in the relatively remote future. But the traditional natural signs were not intended to be applied to such cases, and we can at least conclude for them that interpretation requires a linguistic capacity.

It is not simply this capacity that is a prerequisite for interpreting nearly all the examples used to illustrate the natural signs. A person must also have heard and believed or be able to formulate to himself a specific linguistic generalization in order to be able to interpret them. One who has not heard and believed 'Clouds cause rain' or some equivalent generalization or is not able at least to formulate to himself such a generalization will not, on observing clouds, anticipate the coming rain. The generalization is an essential premiss, even if not explicitly stated, in inferring to what the clouds stand for. A person may not be able to articulate to others the premisses used in predicting the future event; the inference may become habitual and the premisses fade from active memory. Nevertheless, the inference, even if only in a tacit, submerged form, will be used in making the prediction.

These considerations lend substance to Harman's charge (cf. Section 2.5) that there are no important analogies between the traditional natural signs and linguistic expressions as signs. Certainly we do not infer from a linguistic expression and some empirical generalization to what the expression stands for. Suppose someone were to use the single-word sentence 'Red' accompanied by a pointing gesture. Then the speaker's audience would not infer to what 'Red' stands for by means of a generalization such as 'Whenever "Red" is uttered, the color red will appear'. Instead the hearer as a speaker of English would immediately understand the sentence and expect to see the color at the place indicated by the gesture. Indeed, it would be logically impossible for the interpretation of all expressions to require a linguistic generalization by which to infer what they signify. For then the generalization used to make the inference would require for its interpretation a second generalization from which what it signifies would be inferred. This second generalization would require in turn for its interpretation a third generalization, and so on indefinitely. If there is to be a significant analogy between natural signs and linguistic signs, then the former must include only those signs which signify in the same direct, unmediated manner that expressions such as 'Red' do.

We must therefore reject Eco's attempt to state common features of natural and linguistic signs. Natural signs he distinguishes by the Stoic associative-indicative categories.

Linguistic expressions are then distinguished into two classes, those which have a univocal meaning and those with equivocal meaning and subject to different interpretations. The task of 'general semiotics,' Eco announces, is that of tracing 'a single formal structure which underlies all these diverse phenomena, this structure being that of the inference which generates interpretation.' For associative natural signs and univocal sentences the inference is said to be inductive; for indicative signs and equivocal sentences the inference is an abductive one to the best explanation of an effect or best reading of a sentence. The only difference between a 'theory of meaning' for conventional linguistic signs and a 'theory of evidence' is said to be one between the degrees of certitude of the inferences employed: 'If there is a difference, it is not between linguistic and natural signs or between words and symptoms, but rather between *semiotic* and *scientific* inference, or between two kinds of certitude.'[9] But the notion of a 'semiotic inference' is nonsense. All inference is linguistic, involving as it does the rule-governed passage from linguistic premises to a conclusion. Only as rule-governed can it be assessed as either 'correct' or 'incorrect'. As we have seen, we do use an inference in interpreting symptoms and other evidence, but it would be impossible to specify the premises or conclusions of Eco's 'semiotic inference.' It is a fiction introduced to preserve a baseless analogy.

Moreover, to use the term 'sign' in Eco's generic sense that is inclusive of both evidential and linguistic signs would seem to require that we apply such terms as 'stand for', 'signify', or 'means' unequivocally of both. But the application of these terms to the examples of natural signs given by the tradition is clearly borrowed from a supporting empirical generalization in a way dissimilar to their application to linguistic expressions. To state that clouds 'stand for', 'signify', or 'mean' rain is, in effect, to state either the generalization 'Clouds are a probable cause of rain' or 'Usually when clouds occur rain follows'. It is not that the clouds as natural objects have significance or meaning. Rather, they are recognized as instances of the appropriate linguistic generalization, and what we call their 'interpretation' is simply this recognition. More generally, where X and Y are types of natural events or objects, to say 'X signifies Y' is to say 'Whenever (usually when) X is present Y is also.' To say of an instance x of X that it signifies Y ('These clouds mean rain') is also simply to state the supporting generalization and in addition claim x as an instance to which it applies. It is even more obvious that the term 'reference' has no application to evidence. Clouds may signify rain in the sense just outlined, but they clearly do not refer to anything at all. To assign them a reference to the rain is to collapse the crucial distinction between the significance and reference of a sign.

It follows that if 'sign' is to be applied as a generic term it must exclude from its range of application most of the examples of natural signs given in the classical tradition and Peirce's indices. Only those events or objects whose interpretation does not require linguistic mediation are to be included in this restricted range, that is, those which directly signify on the basis of past correlations in experience between tokens of the sign and what it signifies. Are there any such signs encountered in human experience after language acquisition? It seems that there are, and that they are of the variety Price terms 'short-range' signs, e.g. lightning as a sign of thunder or the sight of a candle as a sign of intense heat, where sign and what it signifies are experienced as contiguous or separated by a relatively brief temporal interval. It is more obvious that their interpretation is a central feature of the experiences of lower animals and infants without a linguistic capacity, e.g. the dog for whom the bell is a sign of food, the deer in the forest for whom an odor is a sign of an approaching predator.[10] Such directly interpreted signs we shall term *natsigns* in order to distinguish them from the natural signs of the Medieval tradition. A natsign may be defined as an event having significance for an interpreter which is not produced for the purposes of communication and whose interpretation does not require an inference from a linguistic generalization. Natsigns are thus contrasted with communicated signs, signs used and interpreted in the process of communication. The exact nature of this contrast will be discussed in the next chapter.

But before drawing it we must first consider the extension of natural signs made by Arnauld and Reid to sensory and material images as iconic signs said to signify by virtue of their similarity to the objects they represent. Then we can turn in the last two sections of this chapter to a more exact description of the class of signs that has just been delimited.

3.2 Images

The view that sensory images or sensations are natural signs of objects constitutes the central part of what is called the 'representational theory of perception' first explicitly stated by Locke. The main outlines of this theory are familiar. According to it we do not observe 'external' material objects or events, e.g. tables, rocks, or explosions. Instead, we observe sensory images as 'internal' mental objects causally related to the external ones, e.g. a visual image as the effect of electrical impulses in the central nervous system which are triggered by light irradiation reflected off a surface of an object; an auditory image caused by the sound waves produced by an explosion; a tactile sensation caused by touching an object's surface, etc. These images differ in significant ways from the objects to which they are correlated, and there is no one-to-one correspondence between elements in the image and elements in the object. Nevertheless, there is a structural similarity between the two such that differences in the image correspond to differences in the object, and in this sense the sensory image can be said to be a *representation* or iconic natural sign of the 'external' object. Rather than observing objects, we interpret such signs, and their meaning or significance is simply the respect by which they resemble the objects which cause them. Some philosophers under the influence of Berkeley's analysis of primary qualities, e.g. Reid, deny any resemblance to the correlated object. For them a sensory image is interpreted as only a sign of the bare existence of this object.[11]

This representational theory has been subject to extensive criticisms, the most influential perhaps being those of J.L. Austin and Gilbert Ryle,[12] criticisms sufficiently well-known to save extensive repeating. Having a sensory image or sensation is an aspect of perceiving an object; to see a table requires having a visual image that will be qualitatively different from that which one has when seeing a chair. But the sensory image is not itself an object of perception. If it were, as Ryle argues, to perceive it would require having a second image, which could also then become an object of perception, requiring a third image; and so on indefinitely. If it is objects such as tables and chairs that are perceived and not the sensory images received while perceiving them, then these images are not signs interpreted as either similar to objects or indicators of their existence. Moreover, in order for a sign to be interpreted as representing a given object it would seem necessary for there to be some means of comparing sign with object, e.g. comparing the visual image of a table with the table itself. But obviously under the representational theory no such comparison is possible because the object itself is never observed. For sensory images to be even taken as signs of external existence it would seem also necessary for there to be past correlations between an image and the presence of an object causing it. But again, as Reid concedes in the passage quoted above in Section 2.2, no such correlations could be established if the theory were true, and thus it can only be by what he calls a 'natural kind of magic' that images have significance for an interpreter. This is but to admit that their interpretation is an inexplicable mystery.

By a *material image* we shall mean a naturally occurring image which is a public object observable by more than one individual and causally related to the object of which it is an image. Within this category we include mirror images, shadows, images on television and radar screens, and photographs. Of these mirror images seem to be the most problematic as public objects. Whereas we can locate a shadow on the ground or on the surface of a piece of paper, the location of mirror images is more difficult. They are seen not as on the surface of the mirror but in some sense behind the mirror. But this we assign as their location in 'visual space,' and hesitate to assign them a physical location. Still, we can photograph a mirror image and a mirror image of an object that I see can be seen by anyone else with the same position relative to the mirror as I. In this sense we can classify them as material images. Moreover, they share with the other types the feature of being directly comparable to the objects of which they are images. Just as we can compare a shadow to an object we directly perceive, a TV image on a portable TV to the public event we are observing, and a photograph to the original, so too we can directly compare the mirror image to an object by simply turning around and looking directly at the object mirrored. On the basis of such direct comparisons we can establish systems of projection between image and object, and in this way establish point-to-point correlations that determine the specific respect with which one resembles the other.

All these features seem to differentiate material from sensory images and make plausible the view that, unlike the latter, they are natural signs interpreted as representing the objects to which they are causally related. Moreover, we do not seem to infer to the properties of an object by way of a linguistic generalization of the form 'Such-and-such object is a causally necessary condition for the presence of this type of image.' Instead, the interpretation of a material image as representation is of the 'direct,' unmediated variety characteristic of the interpretation of natsigns.

Nevertheless, the view that material images constitute a species of natsigns is, I think, mistaken. This is obviously so for mirror images. When a person looks into a mirror, he does not see an image and then interpret it as representing himself. Instead, we speak of him 'seeing himself in the mirror.' The expression 'in the mirror' seems simply to mean 'by means of the mirror'. What the person observes is himself, not an image of himself.[13] Of course, at a distance we can see the edges of a mirror and distinguish its outlines from a background. Within this framed outline the mirror image can be seen. But when we observe an object in a mirror these circumstances are ignored, and indeed tend to disappear as we approach a large, clear, translucent mirror whose outlines are beyond our field of vision. The situation is analogous to viewing a distant star through a telescope or a cell through a microscope, with mirrors used to focus and enlarge the image of the object. There are, to be sure, distortions produced by imperfect mirrors and the phenomenon of right-left reversal, both of which can often be corrected only by turning to look directly at the object mirrored. But this is a situation that occurs in cases where we would not speak of representing images. I come from the cold outdoors into a warm room and my eye glasses fog up. The objects around me look blurred and in some cases cannot be distinguished. The person in front of me looks like Jones, but on taking off my glasses I recognize him as Smith. In such cases do we interpret the blurred images as signs representing objects? Of course not. We observe the objects as blurred, not blurred images, and in some cases may misidentify an object and later correct our mistake on the basis of other observations. Likewise, eye glasses have been devised that make their wearers observe objects upside down. Nevertheless, it is still the objects that are observed in this way, not the visual image produced by the distorting lenses.

Similar considerations seem to hold for TV or radar images. We can make these images objects of description, describing them as blurred, fuzzy, clear, or vivid. But when we turn on our TV set to see a football game what we watch is the game itself, not an image of the game interpreted as a representation. There is an obvious difference between seeing the game by going to the stadium and seeing it on television, but these are but different ways of seeing the same event, much as wc can watch a given play with or without the aid of binoculars. What of a taped-delay broadcast of the game? Here it seems the same considerations would apply. What is watched is still the game, not a TV screen image of it interpreted as representing a past event. The fact that the causal sequence initiating with the game itself and terminating with the screen image and finally a visual image produced in the viewer extends over a period of hours, weeks, or even years does not change the fact that the image is a means of observing an event, and is not itself an object of observation. Mistakes occur, of course, in identifying objects seen on screens. A blip on the radar screen may be the occasion for an air controller identifying what happens to be a corporate jet as an airliner as the plane approaches. But such misidentifications occur for observation unaided by instruments, as for a planet misidentified as a star, a mouse as a rat, Jones seen at a distance taken for Smith, etc. In none of these latter cases is misidentification a case of an image failing to match the object it is taken to represent. So too for screen images as a special type of material image.

The sign status of photographs has been the subject of controversy, with some contending that they are a species of iconic natural signs, while others such as Kendall Walton suggesting that we observe objects by means of photos.[14] If our argument so far has been correct, then it is clear that we must endorse Walton's view. If we observe the game by means of television, and even by a delayed broadcast, and not an image as a representation of the game, then there seems no basis for denying that we can also observe the game by means of a film or photo. A photo, of course, has a surface, and can be handled and transported. It can be fine-grained or coarse-grained, heavy or light, etc. A television or film image has itself none of these features, though the screens upon which they are projected do. But there seems no essential difference between viewing a castle by a slide projection image and viewing the castle by a photo. If what we see is the castle in the former case, it would seem to be so also in the latter. To be sure, in ordinary conversation we seem to distinguish the two. To the question, 'Did you see the game between St. Louis and Dallas?', we reply, 'Yes, I saw it on TV' or 'I saw it on video tape.' But if we have never been to England, the question 'Have you seen Marlborough Castle?' would probably evoke 'No, but I have seen a photo of it.' The answer is similar to that we would give to the question 'Did you ever hear Caruso?' 'No, but I have heard a recording of him.' The contrast, however, seems due only to an ambiguity of 'seen' and 'heard.' Interpreted as meaning actually having visited the castle or having attended a Caruso concert, the negative replies are appropriate. But in the more straight-forward senses we normally associate with the verbs it is appropriate to reply 'Yes, I have seen the castle in a photo' and 'Yes, I have heard Caruso on a record.' In both cases the person can claim to have perceived, though in different ways than if he had visited or attended.

Some may contend that the reasoning just given is an instance of a 'slippery slope' argument to an obviously false conclusion by transitions from sensory images to mirror images, television screen images, and finally photos. But it is difficult to see at what stage and why we make the transition from observing objects by means of images to observing images as signs representing objects. Suppose we claim that the transition occurs with TV screen images: we see objects through mirrors, while TV images and photos are natural signs, with the difference between the two due to the interposition for the latter of a medium or device through which the image is produced. But since we observe through binoculars, telescopes, and microscopes, all of which are mechanical devices, this fails to provide a basis for the distinction. It is just as plausible to make the distinction on the basis of whether there is a continuous sequence of events initiating with the object and terminating in the material image. On this basis material images from 'live' TV broadcasts would be distinguished from those from tape-delayed broadcasts and from photos. Similarly, hearing a voice over a long-distance phone cable and satellite transmission would be distinguished from hearing a recording of that voice. Interruption of continuous transmission and storage of information can thus be taken as blocking observation and requiring interpretation of images as signs. But continuous transmission seems an *ad hoc*, arbitrary condition for observation, and fails to accord with distinctions we actually make. We may be unaware that we are watching a game via a tape-delayed broadcast. On learning that this is the case, would we correct our earlier belief that we were in fact watching the game? Obviously not. All that we would be correcting is our belief about *how* we were watching it. Observation can be done in many ways, one of which involves interruption of signal, information storage, and later retrieval.

So far we have rejected sign status for mirror images, TV screen images, and photos. Can we then conclude that no material images function as signs representing objects? I think this would be too hasty. Consider, for example, shadows. The sight of an object and its shadow are present together in our experience. When we see the shadow alone we anticipate the object on the basis of this previous experience. On seeing the object we recognize what was expected, as when we see the shadow of an approaching figure behind us, and then turn around to see a person. No linguistic generalizations seem required for the interpretation of shadows as representations of objects, and indeed they are interpreted by lower animals, as when a squirrel flees at the sight of a hawk's shadow. Shadows thus seem a species of natsigns. Moreover, since resemblance can be recognized between shadows and the objects for which they stand, they should be classified as iconic natsigns.

The interpretation of shadows can be contrasted with that of impressions or traces of objects such as bullet holes, footprints, or fossils in the manner that we contrasted the interpretation of natsigns with the interpretation of classical evidential signs in the previous section. Impressions and traces constitute evidence from which we infer their causes by means of generalizations. To be unaware that fossils are caused by life existing millions of years ago is to be unable to interpret them as traces of this past life. Similarly, a detective must have knowledge of causal generalizations to infer from a footprint or bullet hole to their causes. In interpreting such evidence we not only infer what is its cause, but also what it looked like, since our causal generalizations include information about the respect by which the cause resembles its impression. The use of causal generalizations to make such inferences is, of course, absent when we look at TV images or photos. A person can be totally ignorant of the causal relations between object and the screen image or photo, and still be able to see the object by means of them.[15] Young children and the uneducated are as adept as the trained physicist, just as primitive man could observe objects before knowing about light waves and the mechanisms by which light is transformed to impulses transmitted by the optic nerve to the brain. For some objects in photos we may require a special background, as in determining whether a bone is fractured from an x-ray negative or identifying a particle in a photo of a particle collision. But this is in principle no different from the identification of a bird as a member of a certain species. *All* perceptual identification and description requires a conceptual background, but it does not require knowledge of a cause–effect relation between object and image of the kind required to interpret impressions or traces as evidence of their causes.

The material images we have been discussing differ, then, from shadows as iconic natsigns and traces or impressions as evidence in that they are not interpreted on the basis of correlations in prior experience or linguistic generalizations supported by such correlations. Some may object to our imposing on iconic signs conditions which apply only to those of the non-iconic variety. An iconic sign does not signify the type of object or event with which it has been associated in experience. Instead, it 'shows' its object, where 'showing' is a primitive relation not reducible to others. TV screen images and photos represent things in exactly this way, it can be argued, without their interpretation being based on correlations or linguistic generalizations.[16] This object, however, appeals to a relation which is left totally unexplained. The ability to interpret material images as 'showing' the objection they represent is as mysterious as Reid's 'magical power' from which we were supposed to infer the existence of objects. A shadow can be said to show us its object, for experience informs us of the respect with which shadows resemble objects. Similarly, there is a sense in which a fossil shows us past life or a bullet hole the bullet that produced it. Here causal generalizations allow us to infer from these traces the shapes and sizes of their causes. But the other material images are not interpreted as showing in this manner and no alternative account would seem capable of being given which explains their interpretation.[17]

We shall return to iconic signs later in Section 4.2 where the focus is on the role of iconic comsigns in conveying a speaker's intent. For now our purpose has been simply to restrict further the class of natural signs which can serve as a basis for comparisons to linguistic signs. Besides excluding the classical evidential signs and Peirce's indices, the class of natsigns also excludes the sensory and material images of such philosophers as Reid and Arnauld. With the possible exception of shadows, material images are not signs representing objects but instead means by which objects are observed.

3.3   Natsigns: some basic features

We turn now to our main task, that of specifying those features of natsigns that enable us to compare and contrast them with linguistic signs. As our paradigm linguistic sign we take an utterance of a simple singular indicative sentence with a monadic or one-place predicate, e.g. 'This table is brown' with the demonstrative phrase 'this table' as the singular subject term and 'is brown' as predicate or 'John is short' with a proper noun subject. The principal logical features of the use by a speaker of such sentences and their interpretation by a hearer have been much discussed. Three of them are of special importance for the comparisons we want to make.

1 *Sentences and significance*. A particular utterance is discriminated from background 'noise' as having significance or being meaningful for a hearer by virtue of its being a token or instance of a sentence as a type of expression repeatable on different occasions. The constituent words of the sentence and their combination are governed by conventional rules which both speaker and hearer follow as members of the same speech community. Thus, to understand an utterance of 'This table is brown', the hearer must have learned the rules in English governing the use of the demonstrative 'this' and how to apply

correctly the constituent words 'table' and 'brown.' He or she must also be able to follow the syntactic rules governing the combination of these words plus the appropriate form of the verb 'to be' to form a sentence. How conventional rules governing types of expressions enhance communication will be discussed more fully below in Section 4.2.

2 *Utterances and reference.* In contrast to significance as a function of a rule-governed type, it is the utterance itself together with the particular context in which it is produced that determines its reference. The referent of an utterance of 'This table is brown' is a persistent object as identified by the hearer by means of the subject term 'this table' on the occasion at which the speaker produces the utterance. The spatial orientation of the speaker on that occasion plus perhaps a pointing gesture and eye direction indicates the spatial location of what he intends to refer to by the subject. The subject as used on a different occasion may refer to an entirely different object at a different place. Moreover, the occasion of utterance plus the present tense of the verb fixes temporal boundaries within which the utterance is to be judged true or false. It is the table as referred to now, on the present occasion, that is being described as brown. If it were to be painted another color at some later time, we would not correct what the speaker had said. Where proper nouns occur as subjects, as in 'John is short', the spatial location of the referent is often not directly indicated, though context may serve to indicate which of several individuals named 'John' is being referred to. But verb tense and occasion of utterance again serve to impose temporal boundaries for truth and falsity. The fact that John later grows tall is not grounds for judging the utterance false.

3 *Interpretation.* To be able to interpret an utterance it must have significance for a hearer as a token of a type governed by conventional rules, and he must be able to identify the referent intended by the speaker. The interpretation of the utterance by the hearer is his acceptance or rejection of it as true or false. The verbal expression of this acceptance or rejection is assent or denial. There are two kinds of interpretation. We shall refer to interpretation as *complete* when the hearer identifies the intended referent and judges whether or not the predicate is true of it.[18] This identification and judgment can be of an object directly

present in experience or can be on the basis of memory. Interpretation is *partial* when the hearer accepts the utterance as true, but not on the basis of a judgment of truth. The sole basis is instead a trust in the reliability of the speaker. Our interpretation of most conversational communication would seem to be of this variety, as it is usually pointless to describe to someone objects with which he is either directly acquainted or can readily describe for himself. 'This table is brown', for example, is usually pointless, though 'John is tall' said of an absent John can be informative. For partial interpretation all that is necessary is that the hearer be capable of identifying the referent and judging whether the predicate holds, that is, that he understand the utterance.

When we turn to natsigns such as lightning as a sign of thunder or the sight of a flame as signifying intense heat we readily see that many of the features just listed are absent. As naturally occurring events they are, of course, not used to communicate and hence are not governed by conventional rules. For such a sign to have significance for its interpreter is not for him or her to be able to follow a rule governing the sign as a type. Moreover, there is no object which is the referent of a natsign. To interpret the flash of lightning the interpreter does not first identify some object persisting through time. Instead, there is direct recognition of whether or not the event of thunder followed within the temporal interval it was expected. Finally, in the absence of a conventional rule governing the sign type, to interpret the sign would not seem to accept or reject it as true or false. The term 'true' and 'false' seem applicable only when we can judge compliance or non-compliance with a rule.

Nevertheless, certain basic features of utterance interpretation seem to be present also in the interpretation of natsigns. Only certain events are discriminated from their background as having significance by an interpreter, and, as before for utterances, they are so discriminated by virtue of being tokens of types that have been previously encountered in experience. One seeing lightning for the first time does not interpret it as a sign of thunder. It is only on the basis of prior correlations between the sight of lightning flashes and sounds of thunder that the flash seen on some present occasion signifies thunder. More generally, an event x is a natsign for some interpreter only if it is discriminated as a token of a type of event X which has been correlated in the past experience of the interpreter with occurrences of some other event Y. This latter type of event can then be said to be the significance of x for the interpreter.

An event x cannot be said, however, to refer to a type Y, nor to an occurrence y of Y at some later occasion. Though virtually all sign theorists make this error,[19] this is to confuse the sign's reference with its significance. For an utterance of 'This table is brown', we certainly would not confuse the table as the referent we identify with the utterance's significance, nor would we confuse it with the perception of brown that enables us to judge the utterance as true. We should then not equate the sound of the thunder we hear as the referent of the flash of lightning. In fact, if we are to preserve any analogy with verbal utterances, neither objects nor events can be said to constitute the referents of natsigns. But a token of such a sign can be said to refer to a certain temporal interval or spatial location within or at which the interpreter expects on the basis of prior experience an occurrence of the type of event it signifies. Within a relatively restricted temporal interval after seeing the lightning flash we expect the thunder to follow; if it does not, we recognize the absence, and experience surprise. Similarly, on seeing the flame thrust at us we expect intense heat at the same place as the flame. The occurrence of what is signified by a given sign token we shall term a *significate occurrence*. The spatial-temporal occasion at which we recognize a significate occurrence or non-occurrence we term the sign's *referent occasion*. Because of the psychological limitations discussed in 3.1, this referent occasion will be either spatially contiguous or temporally proximate to the occasion at which the sign is discriminated.

Complete interpretation of a natsign consists in the recognition of a significate occurrence or non-occurrence at the sign's referent occasion. If there is an occurrence y of Y as the type expected, then there is recognition of a significate occurrence; if some other event of type Y' occurs or if there is simply nothing that can be distinguished from the background at the referent occasion, then there is recognition of a non-occurrence. Repeated recognition of non-occurrences has the effect of changing the significance of a sign of type X for the interpreter or replacing it with another sign X' with the same significance. Thus, if events of type Y' rather than Y are recognized as following X, then Y' becomes X's significance. If Y follows only when the more specific event X' occurs, then X' signifies Y, not X. An example of this latter might be our recognizing that so-called 'heat lightning' on a calm summer day is not followed by thunder, while lightning during a storm is. The sign that signifies thunder thus becomes lightning-in-storm rather than simply lightning-in-general. All direct learning from experience involves in this way either the change of significance of a sign of type X or discrimination of a sign of type X' from that of type X as having a given significance. The contrast between the recognition of a significate non-occurrence resulting in such a change and a judgment of falsity should be obvious. If I judge someone's utterance of 'This is brown' false, I revise my estimate of the speaker's reliability. But the significance of 'brown' and that of the sentence as a whole remains a constant, being fixed by the conventions of the language I share with the speaker.[20]

Partial interpretation of natsigns typically occurs when the sign signifies a type of event to which the interpreter has an aversion and he acts in such a way to avoid it. I have an aversion towards the intense heat signified by the sight of the flame. I thus move my hand or step back in order to avoid recognizing a significate occurrence. In such cases there is expectation leading to action, but without recognition. How signs are interpreted as signifying actions will be discussed in the next section.

Though difficult to isolate, the interpretation of natsigns seems to be a feature of adult human experience. It is true that when we see the lightning or the flame we usually identify them as instances of what the words 'lightning' or 'candle' apply to, and it is always possible to infer by way of a linguistic generalization to a linguistic description of what they signify. Nevertheless, we are all familiar with unmediated interpretation. We can be driving a car while thinking of a subject that can only be represented in linguistic terms and still interpret the pot hole ahead as a sign of a rude jolt and swerve to avoid it. This pre-verbal sign interpretation exists parallel with but independently of thinking as a type of interpretation of the verbal. It is the features of this familiar experience we are attempting to describe when we specify the main features of the interpretation of natsigns.

For infants and lower animals lacking a capacity to use

language this interpretation is dominant in experience, and on the basis of what we observe of their behavior we seem justified in describing their interpretation of natsigns in terms with which we describe our own. Thus, we describe the dog as hearing the buzzer and expecting the sight of food. When the food is presented it recognizes an occurrence of what is expected at the sign's referent occasion. If no food is presented, the dog recognizes a significate non-occurrence, and may discriminate in the future features of the buzzer sound (loudness, duration, etc.) which are followed by food from those which are not. In fact, any organism capable of learning from experience would seem to be an interpreter of natsigns, including even the amoeba learning to discriminate substances in its environment which are to be ingested from those to be avoided. By analogy we can apply to such organisms the same psychological terms 'discrimination', 'expectation', and 'recognition' that we apply in describing our own interpretation of natsigns.

The dominant tradition in philosophy, however, would prohibit such psychological descriptions. According to this tradition we can describe the behavior of lower animals and how they respond to given environmental stimuli, but for creatures with which we do not share a common language mental terms have at best a very indefinite application. The main reasons for this view have been well stated by Strawson in defending Kant's restriction of his categorial analysis to human experience:

> Surely infants and non-human animals have experience! – This is not denied. But we must think of how we think, of how we must think, of the experience of such creatures. We have no way of doing so except on a simplified analogy with our own. . . . Any description we can give . . . must be in terms of concepts derived from ours. We can say, if we like, that such ascriptions must, in these thoughts, bear some confused or attenuated or diminished sense. But we must admit that we cannot say what this sense is. . . .[21]

But to the extent that we can describe our own interpretation of natsigns we have words 'to say what it is to be without them,' and can extend such descriptions to creatures who show by their behavior that they share with us this primitive kind of sign interpretation. To deny that we can seems only to cling to a methodological dogma that has dominated philosophy since Descartes.

The difficulties encountered by behavioral semiotic discussed in 2.4 seem to argue against identifying natsigns with stimuli impinging on interpreters' sense organs which evoke overt responses. Indeed, the characteristic 'response' to natsigns interpreted in the way we have been discussing is, as we have seen, a recognition of a significate occurrence or non-occurrence at the referent occasion, and this need not be accompanied by any overt behavioral response.[22] There may be some internal physiological event with which we can correlate or identify this psychological act of recognition, e.g. muscular relaxation or tension or some potentially observable neural event. But then behaviorism's methodological grounds for identifying the sign and its significance with a stimulus and response as events observable 'outside the skin' of the organism disappears. The Berkeleyan alternative to behaviorism is to identify both sign and significate occurrence with phenomenal events, sensory images or sensations with which we are directly aware. That this is unacceptable is clear at least for significate occurrences. These are recognized at a referent occasion to which the interpreter is directed by the sign as an event in its environment. It is the flame perceived as located at a certain place that gives rise to the expectation of intense heat at that place.

The more plausible alternative is to regard the natsign as an environmental event discriminated from a background, with a significate occurrence being an environmental event recognized at a referent occasion. For varying purposes we can describe different aspects of these complex events involving causal transactions between environment and the interpreter interacting with it. For one set of purposes it may be useful to describe the events in terms of the stimuli impinging on the interpreter's sense organs. For others we may describe the neural event that is the effect of the environmental. For still others we may restrict description to the sensory image we are aware of subjectively in immediate experience, as in a description of how bright the flame appears or how loud the thunder sounds. Relationships between these alternative descriptions have become the topic of metaphysical controversy. Is the neural event identical with or causally correlated to the sensory image we are aware of? Can descriptions of sign interpretation formulated in the common sense or 'folklore' terminology of 'discrimination', 'expectation', and 'recognition' we have been employing be regarded as equivalent to or eventually replaceable by theoretical descriptions of causal relations between environmental inputs, internal brain states, and behavioral outputs, and thus patterned on descriptions of information processing by computers? Whatever the intrinsic interest of these questions, it is not the business of semiotic as a discipline to provide answers to them. For semiotic the sign, its significance, and the referent occasion are *logical* elements, and the relations between them are *logical* relations analyzable in the same manner that we analyze the differing logical functions of sentences used in human communication. Just as we can distinguish the differing functions of the subject and predicate of a sentence as used and interpreted without first resolving the mind-body problem, so too the basic elements of sign interpretation can be distinguished and analyzed independently of related metaphysical (and probably unresolvable) problems.

3.4 Dynamic interpretation

So far we have been focusing on a special mode of interpretation in which a natsign x of type X is discriminated as having as significance an event of type Y which is recognized as occurring or not occurring at a referent occasion. We shall refer to this as *cognitive interpretation*. As we have seen, such interpretation is partial when the sign gives rise to an action which has the effect of avoiding a significate occurrence, as when we withdraw our hand to avoid the intense heat of the flame. In contrast to this, the mode of interpretation in which the sign is taken as a sign of a type of action which can be either performed or not performed, we shall follow Peirce in referring to as *dynamic interpretation*.[23]

The paradigm linguistic sign as the object of dynamic interpretation is the singular imperative used in ordinary conversation, e.g. 'Close the door' or 'Don't hit Peter,' in which the singular terms 'this door' and 'Peter' function as subject terms used by the speaker to refer to objects and the remainder of the sentence consists of predicates signifying types of actions directed or oriented towards these objects. On identifying the objects to which he takes the speaker to intend to refer, the hearer decides whether or not to obey or disobey a particular utterance of the imperative, a decision in which aversion to punishment or desire for reward are often motivating factors. It is such decisions to obey or disobey that constitute the dynamic interpretation of an imperative utterance, just as acceptance as true or denial as false constitute the cognitive interpretation of an utterance of an indicative. One who is unable to determine what constitutes obedience or disobedience fails to understand the significance or meaning of a given imperative.

As before for cognitive interpretation, we must be careful not to assume that all natural events giving rise to actions are primitive analogues of imperatives as linguistic signs. Typically in human experience natural events are related to actions by way of a mediating inference. Though not classified as natural signs by the tradition, we do speak of an impending storm as a sign to the housewife to take in the clothes, an acute pain in a patient's lower right abdomen as a sign for the doctor to remove his or her, appendix, and a prolonged drought as a sign to the investor to invest in grain futures. In all such cases the observer of the 'sign' employs a complex practical inference to infer to the action that should be performed in order to avoid or bring about a certain state of affairs. In the case of the housewife the sign is a *warning* that a certain action ought to be performed as a means of avoiding a state of affairs to which she has an aversion. The inference used is a practical inference which can be formulated as:

I don't want wet clothes
My not taking in the clothes is sufficient for their
    becoming wet if there is a thunderstorm
There will be a thunderstorm
_____

I ought to take in the clothes

More generally, let us take E^* to be a 'bad' state of affairs to which a person has an aversion and M an action which is a means of avoiding E* if circumstance C obtains. To interpret C as a warning to do M is to use an inference of the form:

I don't want E*
My not doing M is sufficient for E* if C
C obtains
_____

I ought to do M

To report the coming storm is thus to state a premiss from which a requirement to perform the action is inferred.

Where C is a circumstance for performing an action M which is necessary to attain a wanted state of affairs or end E, we interpret C as an opportunity for E. The form of inference used is then:

I want E
My doing M is necessary to attain E if C
C obtains
_____

I ought to do M

Thus, the investor interprets the drought as an opportunity to invest in grain futures, reasoning that such an investment is necessary to attain a profit under drought conditions.[24] To apply the term 'sign' to the circumstance C of both this and the previous example is to destroy any possible analogy to imperative sentences. While an imperative directly expresses a type of action that is to be performed, it is the *report* of the circumstance as it occurs in the context of a practical inference which allows an inference to a *statement* of an obligation. The circumstance C 'means' the action M in the sense that it is a premiss from which the prudential obligation to do M can be inferred. With such inferences those with a linguistic capacity can anticipate actions in the distant future and at remote places as a means to pursuing even more remote ends.

In contrast, the referent occasion of a natsign as an object of dynamic interpretation is spatially contiguous or temporally proximate to the sign. It is here and now that I withdraw my hand on seeing the approaching flame. If I fail to withdraw it in the near future from the place at which I see the flame, I expect the painful heat. A type of action Z as the dynamic significance of a particular natsign x of type X must be performed at this referent occasion if the benefit associated with it is to be attained or (as in the case of the flame), a harm avoided. Typically this referent occasion coincides with that for the sign as the object of cognitive interpretation, the occasion at which an occurrence of type Y as its cognitive significance is expected. The place from which I must withdraw my hand is the place at which I expect the intense heat I want to avoid.

As before for cognitive interpretation, the dynamic significance of a natsign can change over time. Suppose that action-type Z is the significance of a natsign of type X for an interpreter I at t_1. Then if on subsequent occasions particular performances of Z fail to avert what is painful or secure what is enjoyable, then either X will signify for I at some later time t_2 some other action-type Z' which does have these effects or I will learn to discriminate some other event of type X' for which Z is the significance. Thus we learn to react to our environment. The contrast to imperatives as conventional linguistic signs is clear. Whether or not the child obeys utterances of the imperative 'Clean up your room' will depend largely upon whether the parent follows up compliance with rewards and non-compliance by punishment. But these rewards and punishments do not alter the meaning of the sentence; only the authority of the parent is changed, whether strengthened or weakened. The significance of the sentence remains fixed by conventional rules governing its constituent words and their combination. In contrast, it makes no sense to apply the terms 'obey' and 'disobey' of natsigns as objects of dynamic interpretation. Like 'true' and 'false' they have application only to conventional signs in the context of communication.

The dynamic interpretation of natsigns is a familiar part of our everyday experience. The batter ducking to avoid the fast ball aimed at his head, the driver swerving to avoid the pot hole, the fisherman jerking his rod at the feel of a tug – all are reacting to their environment in a way which seems to involve no linguistic mediation. They do not identify some event in order to infer from the premisses of a practical inference to an action. Instead, they simply perform an action directly signified by what they see or feel on that occasion. Such interpretation is just as obviously a part of the experience of lower animals, and perhaps easier to isolate there than in the experience of language users such as ourselves. We can readily identify natsigns with what Skinner terms the 'controlling stimulus' (cf. 2.4) in the standard examples of instrumental learning. In such learning, as we have seen, a controlling stimulus, e.g. a buzzer, elicits a response or operant which is then subject to positive or negative reinforcement. As various types of controlling stimuli are selectively reinforced the animal learns to modify its responses. Thus, if loud tones of the buzzer followed by a pressing of a bar by a rat are rewarded by food pellets, while soft tones are not, the rat learns to discriminate loud tones from soft and respond only to the former. Through what psychologists call 'stimulus generalization' the animal tends to respond to any buzzer sound, loud or soft. Selective reinforcement brings about the discrimination of a certain loudness, as the natsign signifying for its interpreter the rewarded response. The basic features of such controlled laboratory situations would seem to be present in all situations in nature where organisms learn to discriminate signs from an environmental background and modify responses in order to satisfy their wants.

Many will object on metaphysical grounds to any comparison between an action performed in compliance with an imperative and a response made to a controlling stimulus. An utterance of an imperative, it will be said, provides a *reason* for the action, but the stimulus is a *cause*, along with the previous reinforcement schedule, of the response as a movement of the organism. The imperative plus promises of rewards and threats of punishment may provide reasons *for* a person performing the action that is signified. But a stimulus as a cause in conjunction with the internal physiological state of an organism can only be part of an explanation of *why* it behaved as it did or a basis for predicting future behavior. Another contrast may be cited. We speak of a person 'deciding' whether or not to obey an imperative, or of his or her 'choosing' to obey or disobey. But such terms seem to have no application to lower organisms capable of instrumental learning. After a series of trials an amoeba learns to reject a piece of glass before ingesting it. It is nonsense to speak of the amobea 'deciding' or 'choosing' to reject the glass. It is equally nonsensical to describe in these terms a rat's pressing a lever in response to a buzzer or even a chimpanzee pressing a button on seeing a visual display to receive a reward. If our psychological descriptions of persons obeying imperatives are so different, it will be argued, then there is no basis for an analogy to dynamic interpretation of natsigns by lower animals.

Of these contrasts, we must concede only that between psychological descriptions. It is true that terms such as 'decide' and 'choose' have applicability only to language users. We decide and choose on the basis of deliberation in which we use a practical inference to infer what should be done. Obviously, to formulate the premises and conclusion of such an inference requires a linguistic capacity which lower animals and infants lack. Once having inferred a conclusion that action Z should be performed we normally resolve 'I shall do Z' and form an intention. A being incapable of inferring this conclusion and formulating the resolutive sentence is not one to which such decisions and choices can be ascribed. The situation parallels that for belief ascriptions. One principal basis for ascribing a belief of interpreter I is I's assertion or assent to a sentence expressing the content of that belief. If I sincerely asserts or assents to the sentence 'It is raining,' then by what Kripke terms the 'Disquotational Principle' we can ascribe to I the belief that it is raining.[25] By the 'Converse Disquotational Principle' we can infer that if I believes that it is raining then (assuming I is aware of what he believes) I will assent to the sentence 'It is raining.' Where we only have non-verbal behavior on which to base belief ascriptions we commonly ask whether this behavior and the situation in which it occurs is of the type that would accompany our assent to indicative sentences expressing the belief's content. This conceptual link between belief ascriptions and uses of sentences precludes saying of a dog that it believes it is raining or believes that it will get food on hearing a bell.[26] Instead, we ascribe a more general term such as 'expectation' that lacks this conceptual link to language. It should be noted that for human dynamic interpretation of natsigns we usually withhold using the terms 'decide' and 'choose'. The batter seeing the ball aimed at his head or the driver seeing the pot hole do not decide. But they do intentionally duck or swerve, just as the rat can be said to intentionally press the bar on hearing the buzzer, without also deciding or choosing to do so.

But from these considerations no metaphysical distinction can be inferred to exist between the dynamic interpretations of imperatives and natsigns. It is important to note that if a given event evokes a reflex response it is not to be regarded as a natsign and an object of interpretation. Someone shines a bright light in my face and I blink. The bright light is no more a sign to me of blinking than food particles are a sign to the dog of salivation or an electric shock administered to its paw a sign of a lifting response. What distinguishes these from responses to natsigns is they are not modifiable on the basis of future experience. We cannot learn not to blink at the bright flash. The responses to all natsigns are, in contrast, subject to modification. Only beings capable of learning from experience and discriminating natsigns on the basis of pleasure and pain experienced after past responses can be regarded as their interpreters.[27]

Once this distinction is made, there is no difficulty in applying causal terminology to both natsigns and imperatives. The sergeant shouts to the sitting recruit 'Attention!'. Is the utterance of the imperative the cause of the recruit's jumping up or its reason? Both would seem appropriate accounts, though in the absence of any deliberation we would probably be more inclined to cite the utterance as a cause. Is the buzzer the cause of the rat's bar pressing or its reason? Here we would probably exclude the account in terms of reasons, since the rat is incapable of deliberating by means of a practical inference. The use of causal terminology in both cases carries with it no metaphysical implications. The rat's interpretation of the natsign is 'mental' in the same sense as the recruit's interpretation of the utterance of the imperative. Characterizing both in this way is justified on the basis of the logical functions of the signs as objects of interpretation, logical functions which are in marked contrast to the functions of a cause of a reflex response. As we have seen, which special mental ascription we apply will depend on the level of sign, whether a natsign or linguistic sign. We can also give a 'physical' description of a sequence of events beginning with the occurrences of both signs and terminating in the responses of jumping up and bar pressing. There is no mental–physical distinction between human dynamic interpretation and sub-human. Both are mental and physical, depending on the purposes with which we want to describe them.

This concludes our discussion of the level of signs which is most primitive in both a logical and evolutionary sense. As signs without internal subject–predicate structure and without the features of signs used with intent to communicate, natsigns are logically primitive. Their basic features of referring an interpreter as tokens to a referent occasion and signifying as tokens of a type an event or action are present in all signs of higher levels of complexity, but there are features of these more complex signs which are absent in them. Natsigns are also primitive in the sense that organisms with the capacity to interpret them in fact evolved before those with higher-level capacities. Indeed, we can speculate that evolution *must* follow a progression in which the capacity to interpret natsigns is temporally prior. The logical simple–complex distinction as applied to signs thus coincides with one between earlier and later developmental stages.

4 COMMUNICATION

The previous chapter has sought to establish natsigns as a category of signs exclusive of the traditional natural signs and at least most instances of material images. In this chapter the focus is on signs used for communication between members of a community. In the first section we employ Grice's account of 'non-natural' meaning to demarcate signs used to communicate from natsigns, and then in the next section set forth conditions for conventional signs. In the third section are discussed the basic features of signals as a type of communicated sign lacking subject-predicate structure. Finally, the attempt is made to specify those features of human languages which distinguish them from all other types of possible communication systems.

4.1 Communicative intent

One of the defining characteristics of natsigns is that they are not produced with communicative intent. In this respect they can be contrasted with what we shall term *comsigns*, signs that are produced with communicative intent and interpreted as such by their interpreters.[1] The bristling of the hairs on the back of a dog may be a sign for some interpreters of imminent attack through past correlations in experience between the bristling and attack movements by the animal. As an object of dynamic interpretation it may then be a sign of withdrawal to avoid the attack. Assuming no linguistic mediation, we would then characterize the bristling as a natsign. It is not something which the dog does, but a reflex response by the dog to a threatening situation. In contrast, a snarl by the dog warning of imminent attack *may* be characterized in a different way. If we determine that the dog intends the snarl as a warning and a means of forestalling combat by bringing about withdrawal, then we would characterize it as a comsign, a sign produced with communicative intent. But if the snarl is like the bristling in being the dog's reflex response to its situation, we would judge it a natsign. Though we can use examples such as this to indicate how comsigns are demarcated as a distinct class of signs, the key term 'communicative intent' remains vague and leaves indefinite the natsign–comsign distinction. Exactly what are the conditions for characterizing a given event as a comsign? How does the natsign–comsign distinction differ from the traditional distinction between natural and conventional signs? Some philosophers have questioned the ascription of intentions to lower animals. Are there behavioral criteria by which we can distinguish an action producing a comsign from a reflex movement by an organism which may be interpreted as a sign but does not involve communication? These are some of the questions to which we now turn.

An important aid in making explicit the conditions for communication is H.P. Grice's theory of what he calls 'non-natural' meaning. Grice wants to distinguish cases in which a person interprets natural events and objects as meaningful from cases of interpretation of comsigns (or what he calls 'utterances') used to communicate.[2] Spots on a patient may mean for the doctor that he has measles, a person's handkerchief at the scene of the crime may mean to the detective that he is the murderer, and a policeman standing in the way may mean to the motorist to drive to the side of the road. But the sense in which these phenomena have 'meaning' is clearly different from that occurring when a person gestures to indicate someone is sick (e.g. choking himself with his hands and pointing to him), someone draws for the detective a person shooting the victim, or the policeman waves the motorist to the side of the road. The gestures and the drawing are used with communicative intent and are interpreted as such by those to whom they are addressed, and are thus comsigns.

Grice formulates three necessary and sufficient conditions for an event x being a comsign:

(i) A communicator C intends x to produce some effect E (e.g. a belief, an action) on an interpreter I;

(ii) C intends I to recognize the intention of (i); and

(iii) I's recognition of the intention of (ii) is a reason for the effect E on I.

All three conditions in Grice's view are necessary for *x* being a comsign. Suppose that a person A leaves a suspect's handkerchief at the scene of the crime intending to induce a belief in a detective B that the suspect is guilty. Then A may have made evidence available to B with the intention specified in (i), but he is clearly not openly communicating with B. Similarly, a policeman may stand in front of another's car intending to produce the effect of his driving to the side, but this is again not communication. Failing the satisfaction of condition (ii), neither the handkerchief nor the standing are comsigns. Moreover, it is at least conceivable that A may leave the handkerchief at the scene of the crime knowing that B is looking on, and intend that B recognize his intention of inducing belief in another's guilt. But this will clearly not be a reason for B's holding this belief, and in fact will normally have a quite opposite effect. Hence, condition (iii) is also necessary. In contrast, it seems that a drawing by A for B showing the shooting and the waving by the policeman to pull over do satisfy all three conditions, and for this reason we regard them as comsigns. The drawing is intended to induce belief and A intends this intention to be recognized. If B does believe A, it will be at least in part due to the recognition of this intention. Similarly, the waving by the policeman is intended to produce the effect of having the motorist drive to the side, and he intends this intention to be recognized. If the motorist obeys, it is partly due (he may also fear fines or imprisonment, etc.) to the recognition of the policeman's intention.

It is important to see that the class of objects and events Grice is distinguishing as comsigns does not include natsigns, and hence his distinction is not that which we are seeking. The examples he cites having 'natural' meaning – the spots, the handkerchief, and a host of other examples by him and commentators on his theory – have been almost invariably examples of evidence which have 'meaning' only in the derivative sense of requiring prior knowledge of linguistic generalizations such as 'Measles cause spots' or 'Handkerchiefs are usually dropped only by their owners at places they have been'. To interpret these 'signs' is, in fact, to use an inference in which these generalizations are an essential premiss.[3] Grice has thus used the traditional natural signs as one term of the contrast he seeks to draw. But as we saw in Section 3.1, this is not a contrast in terms of which we can retain a significant analogy to linguistic signs, and the sense in which his natural signs have 'meaning' differs from that for comsigns in much more than the lack of certain communicative intentions.

We can, however, readily adapt Grice's conditions to our distinction between natsigns and comsigns. Every natural event with unmediated significance for an interpreter that does not occur as the consequence of some agent's actions will, of course, be a natsign by virtue of the failure of Grice's condition (i). But conditions (ii) and (iii) also seem necessary. We can imagine someone attempting to manipulate the environment of another, much as the experimenter in animal or infant learning experiments pairs one type of event with that of another or provides a schedule of reinforcements for responses relative to a given controlling stimulus. Let us suppose a subject B who has experienced on a number of occasions a pairing of a buzzer tone with a flash of light on a screen, and suppose that our manipulator A produces a buzzer tone intending to induce in B the expectation that the flash of light will occur. We can also suppose that A intends B to recognize this intention, making himself visible to B, pressing the buzzer signal before him, and glancing at the screen. It will still not follow that B will expect the flash of light there because of the recognition of A's intention. He will instead expect the flash only because of the correlation in past experience between the sign and what it signifies. A gets B to expect the flash, but does not, I think we would agree, communicate with B. Because of the failure of condition (iii), the buzzer sound is not a comsign. Similar considerations hold for manipulation of natsigns to bring about actions. An infant B can be trained by A to perform a task on hearing a buzzer with suitable rewards, and A can then make evident to B this intention and have it recognized. But it would seem that the dynamic significance of the buzzer and the performance of the action is solely a function of the previous training; the present recognition of intention is irrelevant to it.

A number of writers have questioned the sufficiency of Grice's three conditions for a comsign. Examples have been produced showing that a person A can make evidence available to another with intentions (i) and (ii) and producing the effect of (iii), and yet because of an intended deception be not openly communicating with B. Moreover, attempts to produce a fourth condition have been met with examples of other deceptions showing its insufficiency; a fifth condition produces even more subtle deceptions; and so on without apparent end.[4] But it seems that such examples are applicable only to evidence made available with intent to deceive, and are not possible for natsigns. There are many intended actions that we can perform, including making available evidence, and the intended effects on others can be complex. It is perhaps unreasonable to suppose that we can state criteria for distinguishing the results of all these actions from comsigns. It is sufficient for the purposes of semiotic that we be able to distinguish comsigns from natsigns as a different category of *signs*, and this Grice's conditions enable us to do.

There are, however, some minor modifications in Grice's account that must be made. As Strawson notes, often a person can communicate with another with a 'take it or leave it' attitude, intending no specific effect by his or her utterance, as I might say 'It will rain tomorrow', not caring whether a hearer believes me.[5] In such cases we can widen our sense of 'effect' to include the other's understanding of what we say. We will at least always intend to be understood and intend this intention to be recognized. It may also turn out that our intended effect is not produced, contrary to what seems implied by Grice's condition (iii). I may intend to be believed when I say 'It will rain', but the other may not believe me.[6] Here we can reword the condition to state that the other B must recognize my intention to produce an effect (e.g. belief), and *if* that effect *were* produced, B's recognition would be at least a partial reason for it. Incorporating this counterfactual and making explicit the fact that the conditions are applied only to signs and not to evidence or other intended results of actions, we have the following reformulation:

A sign *x* is a comsign if and only if:
(1) *x* is produced by a communicator C with the intent of producing an effect E on some interpreter I; as
(2) C intends that I recognize the intention of (1); and

(3) I recognizes this intention, and if E were produced on I, I's recognition of the intention of (2) would be a reason for E.

These conditions can be regarded as an explication of the vague phrase 'produced with communicative intent and interpreted as such,' used initially to characterize comsigns. A *degenerate comsign* can be characterized as a sign satisfying only conditions (1) and (2) and distinguished from non-degenerate or *proper comsigns* satisfying all three conditions. The signs produced by a manipulator intending his intention to be recognized are thus degenerate comsigns. Natsigns can then be distinguished as signs which are neither degenerate nor proper comsigns and would include signs satisfying only condition (1).

We began this discussion with Mead's distinction between the bristling of a dog's hairs as a sign of imminent attack and a dog's snarl as what Mead calls a 'vocal gesture.' Ethologists studying animal behavior in the wild have recorded a wide variety of signaling displays employed in courtship, mating, defense of territory, food gathering, etc. Can we apply conditions (1) to (3) to distinguish those displays which are comsigns from those which are either natsigns or fail to be objects of interpretation? Much of this display behavior seems to be like the bristling of the dog's hairs in consisting of reflex responses to environmental stimuli and being a function of innate structures that have evolved in a species through the pressures of natural selection. The courtship 'dance' of the male stickleback in the presence of a female, for example, appears to be a sequence of responses to stimuli produced by movements of the female. In such cases there is no intentional action, and thus necessarily no comsign. Moreover, such displays often act as what R.A. Hinde calls 'social releasers' triggering apparently reflex responses in other organisms.[7] Such reflex responses are not the result of sign interpretation, and thus the display is neither a comsign nor a natsign. Other behavior seems just as obviously to involve communicative intent. E.W. Menzel in his studies of young chimpanzees has observed how a captive chimpanzee will lead others to a hidden treasure (e.g. trinkets or food) by glances, beckoning head and hand gestures, and even pulling to the site.[8] These glances and gestures would seem to be comsigns for exactly the same reason as are the hand gestures of the policeman directing the driver to pull to the side of the road. But between these extremes there are gradations. For them it is far from obvious what behavioral criteria we should apply in deciding in particular cases whether conditions (1) to (3) obtain.

Condition (1) requires in part that a comsign be intentionally produced and not a reflex response. Intentionality, in turn, seems to require that an organism learn to produce the comsign, and that innate structures and present environmental stimuli not be in themselves a causally sufficient condition for it. Studies cited by Hinde indicate that displays for some species appear in individuals reared in isolation, and are therefore innate. This would certainly include the highly stereotyped displays of insects such as ants and the dances of Von Frisch's honey bees. But others, e.g. the posturing behavior of gulls, require a social environment and seem to be acquired by imitation of other members of the community. Still other displays are acquired by a learning process other than imitation, 'including perception of the individual's own movements and vocalizations.'[9] Whether a display is intended would also seem determined by whether it is subject to modification if it fails to fulfill an animal's goals. A dog may scratch at the door as a means of being let in by its master. If not let in, it may then resort to barking and whining, thus modifying its behavior and allowing us to judge the scratching as an intentionally produced comsign. In contrast, most animal displays in the wild seem to exhibit no such modification, though often, as Hinde notes,[10] the frequency of a display will be a function of its reinforcement.

But condition (1) requires also that an effect on some interpreter be intended, and condition (2) adds that this effect be intended by the communicator to be recognized. Ethologists seem to be claiming both requirements are fulfilled when they speak of a given signaling display as having the property of 'directedness,' its being directed towards or targeted on one or more interpreters, rather than simply being emitted in the absence of a social context. Condition (3), in turn, requires that an interpreter perceive itself as the intended target of a display and that its response to it will not be a reflex response to a triggering stimulus. Whether all or even some of these conditions are fulfilled is questionable. W.J. Smith thinks that they may be for domesticated animals and higher primates in contact with humans. But in other cases he is doubtful:

If animals do attempt to maximize the effectiveness with which
their display behavior serves their goals, . . . it is not usually
obvious in the field . . . in natural circumstances it often
appears as if most animals perform their displays whenever an
appropriate set of circumstance arises, whether or not the
displays appear to be necessary or effective – as if the displays
were more or less automatic responses. Further, in natural
circumstances each participant does not usually appear to
perceive itself as the target of another's signaling, as conversing
humans do, although it might be very difficult for an observer
to demonstrate this.[11]

Hinde, in contrast, is more circumspect on the question of
communicative intent for these displays, holding that 'there is a
gradation of the complexity of goal-directed behavior and hence
perhaps of intentionality.'[12] Hinde thus seems to admit at least
some forms of degenerate comsigns among sub-human species.
This is perhaps left open also by Smith with his qualifications of
'often', 'more and less,' and 'usually.'

Whether all or some of conditions (1) to (3) are satisfied is, I
think, only partly an empirical question. The studies of the
ethologists can determine the extent to which given signaling
displays are innate or learned and whether their production is
modifiable goal-directed behavior. But the term 'intend' used in
stating these conditions is one we ascribe to other persons on the
basis of behavioral criteria that we are all able to apply in a wide
range of cases without hesitation. Ethologists inform us of
similarities and dissimilarities between animal display behavior
and human communicative behavior. But then it remains a
matter of *deciding* whether the similarities present warrant our
extending the term 'intend' to sub-human forms. Current practice
seems to indicate that we have decided in favor of some
extensions. The stereotyped behavior of insects and fish and
many displays of birds may be sufficiently different to warrant
withholding the term and denying the use of comsigns. But on
the other hand, certain gestures and vocalizations of higher
primates seem similar enough to warrant our concluding
conditions (1) to (3) are fulfilled. Between these extremes are all
the cases where a decision still remains to be made.

4.2 Conventional signs

Grice's theory of the meaning of a comsign consists of two parts. It is primarily a statement of conditions by which a given event can be distinguished as a comsign. We have just seen how these conditions can be adopted as a means of distinguishing comsigns from natsigns. But Grice wants to do more. He also claims that the meaning or significance that a given comsign x has for an interpreter I is what I recognizes a communicator C as intending to mean by x on a given occasion. This stronger thesis will obviously not hold of conventional linguistic signs. I may say to another 'This book is blue' and intend to mean that the book in front of us is red. Moreover, my listener may recognize my intention, realizing that there has been a slip of the tongue or that I am deliberately substituting 'blue' for 'red'. Still, the meaning of 'blue' as it occurs in the sentence uttered is not what I intend. Grice's reply is to distinguish the 'occasion' meaning of a comsign from its 'timeless' meaning.[13] When 'blue' was first introduced into the English language its meaning was its intended meaning on that occasion. But as a part of a shared language its meaning in sentence contexts is what speakers of that language usually intend. Timeless meaning thus becomes established out of repetitions of comsigns with occasion meaning. Since my intended meaning of 'blue' differs from what others usually intend, its meaning on that occasion diverges from its timeless meaning. It is this latter we have in mind when we conclude that the word's meaning for the listener is not what I intend.

Grice's notion of occasion meaning forces us to revise drastically the contrast made in Section 3.3 between the reference and significance of a sign. There we said that while the referent occasion is indicated by a natsign as a token, the sign has significance for an interpreter as a token of a type correlated with significate occurrences on prior occasions. But for a comsign to have occasion meaning, it must have this meaning for an interpreter solely as a token that the interpreter relates to what is recognized to be intended by the communicator on the occasion of use. Suppose a person utters a hissing sound, intending to indicate that a snake is nearby – it is this unique sound, independent of others like it which, according to Grice, has occasion meaning.

Should we regard comsigns of this kind as having significance in a radically different way from that for natsigns? There are several reasons for thinking we should not. A hissing sound is initially a natsign for us of a nearby snake by virtue of prior correlations in experience between it and the sight of a snake. Someone can reproduce this noise, and a listener can recognize the intention to indicate a snake. But it is not the intention which endows the sound with significance. Its significance is derived from the fact that it is discriminated by the listener as of the same type as the naturally occurring sound. Recognizing the communicator's intention is essential for interpreting the sound as a comsign, but this recognition does not determine the sign's significance. Similarly, the spontaneous cries of infants evoke in their parents what seem to be at least partially innate responses of aid or holding shared by almost all species of mammals. At some stage in its development an infant can control these cries and produce comsigns with the intent of receiving affection, aid, etc. On recognizing such an intention for the first time a parent does not discover the significance of a particular cry. Instead, the comsign as an object of dynamic interpretation has the significance of the earlier involuntary cry as a token of this type. As for the hissing sound, there is direct transference from a natural event with significance.

Not all comsigns, of course, have significance by virtue of such transferences. But where they do not they seem usually to be either conventional signs or similar to such signs. Usually, where an intentionally produced sound or gesture is totally unrelated to a convention and does not receive its meaning through natural transference, we regard it as meaningless. Consider a lunatic making the sound 'blurbah' and pointing to a chair. If he were to intend by his utterance to mean a chair and we were able successfully to recognize this intention, it does not at all follow that his utterance has significance for us. In fact, we would say that his utterance or babbling lacked significance, was a mere noise.[14] The fact that he intended it to have a certain meaning does not require it to have that meaning for those recognizing this intention, contrary to Grice's theory. A person may be a host for a dinner at which there is a guest not speaking his language. He motions with palms down, and the guest recognizes his intention of having him sit down. Surely this gesture has occasion meaning! Not at all. Gestures such as this would seem to acquire their significance by virtue of conventions that cross linguistic boundaries. It is because this gesture, or one similar to it, is used in his own country that the foreign guest would be able to interpret it. Where cultural conventions diverge there is failure of communication. In Oriental cultures the gesture beckoning to approach is made with the palm facing the addressee; in the West beckoning is done with the palm facing the gesturer. Traveling in Japan I might recognize a palm-facing gesture as intended to have me approach. But for me this gesture, this particular hand movement, has the meaning of a bidding farewell as a token of a type used in my culture. It does not have its intended meaning, though the gesture may acquire it for me as I learn the conventions of this different culture.

Iconic comsigns interpreted as representing objects by virtue of a similarity to them pose a special problem. A may help B park his car by spreading his hands apart the length that B's car is from the curb, perform a jogging motion indicating that he wants B to jog, or produce a drawing of a snake and point to a nearby location. Here it seems B does not interpret the gesture, motion, or drawing by discriminating them as tokens similar to others of the same type. Instead, interpretation requires B to recognize particular sign tokens as similar to the spatial relation, action, and object they are intended by A to represent. In such cases, I think, we must conclude that the respect by which B recognizes A is intending the comsigns to be similar to what they represent does constitute the meaning or significance of the comsigns. But we must realize how special these cases are, certainly not ones on which to base a general theory of meaning applicable to all comsigns. In fact, even iconic comsigns such as drawings (including maps and diagrams) and gestures tend to be conventionalized, and then tend to become less similar to the objects or actions they represent. Once conventionalized the intentions with which they are used by communicators become irrelevant to their significance, as for the palms down motion of the host. The iconic comsign seems to be principally a device by which this process of conventionalization is begun. By uttering an arbitrary sound frequently enough in the presence of snakes a person can establish it for another as a sound with significance. But this process can be shortened by simply producing an iconic representation or a hissing sound as a transferred natsign. Once significance is established, the comsign can be modified in such a way as to lose some of the sensible features that enabled the initial interpretation.[15]

So far we have set forth a number of sub-classifications of signs. Comsigns have been distinguished from natsigns with respect to communicative intent and divided into two sub-classes. Proper comsigns are those produced by a communicator C with the intent of bringing about an effect on an interpreter I and with the intent to have this intention recognized, and are those for which I's recognition of C's intentions would be a reason for the effect if it were brought about. Degenerate comsigns are those produced with communicative intent by C but for which either I fails to recognize that intent or this recognition would not be a reason for the intended effect being brought about. Proper comsigns can in turn be sub-divided into non-conventional and conventional signs. Included within the non-conventional class are iconic signs with occasion meaning (a gesture, drawing, etc.), and signs whose significance is transferred from natsigns (the hissing sound, an infant's intentional cry). This is obviously not a neat dichotomous classification without overlaps. Degenerate comsigns can also be classified with respect to conventionality and iconicity. Iconic signs can acquire, as we have seen, the features of conventional signs when used with frequency. The classification is useful, however, for specifying the central features of those signs contrasted with conventional comsigns used in typical communication situations.

But to establish the contrast we need also to specify the distinctive features of conventional signs. The classical view was that a convention is an historical agreement reached by decree or stipulation, 'determined by the lawgivers,' as the Stoics said of the torch and bell, or by consensus, as Augustine says may occur (cf. 2.1 and 2.2). In science those making discoveries are indeed usually accorded the status of 'lawgivers' and allowed the privilege of introducing a new technical term and stipulating its meaning. But for the vast majority of expressions governed by linguistic conventions no such agreement is reached. Linguists inform us that one of the most powerful agencies for linguistic change are children and adolescents as they modify existing syntax and introduce slang words. But there is obviously no agreement reached at some period in time to introduce these changes. Instead, the practice of using novel expressions spreads by insensible degrees to wider and wider segments of the linguistic community.

As an alternative to this classical view David Lewis describes a convention as an existing behavioural regularity based on the expectations and preferences of the members of a community.[16] A coordination problem arises for Lewis when there is a shared end within a community which can only be attained if all members behave in similar ways. A solution to the problem is reached when the members establish a pattern of common behavior which in fact leads to the attainment of the end. For some coordination problems it will be a matter of indifference to members of the community which of a number of alternative behavior patterns becomes established. An individual of the group behaves in accordance with a specific pattern that has been established because he or she expects on the basis of past practice that everyone else will also do so and prefers that they do as a means to attaining the end to which the behavioral regularity is a means. A convention, according to Lewis, is just such a specific regularity of behavior.

A regularity R is a convention for this regularity theory, then, if and only if:

(a) everyone conforms to R;
(b) everyone expects everyone else to conform;
(c) everyone prefers to conform to R on the condition that others do, since R is a solution to a coordination problem P.

Condition (c) implies that there are other alternative solutions besides R to P; if there were not, it would not seem possible for a person to prefer to conform on the condition that others do. Thus, driving in safety is a shared end within a given country to which all driving on the same side of the road is a necessary means. It is a matter of indifference whether all drive on the left (as in Great Britain) or on the right, but the citizens of a given country conform to the prevailing practice, whatever it may be, with the expectation that others will do so also. Similar considerations hold of patterns of linguistic behavior. Members of a community share in common the want for economical, efficient means of communication on an indefinite variety of topics, and for this, use of a language with a lexicon and syntactic rules governing the combination of elements of the lexicon into sentences is a prerequisite. What lexicon and what rules are used may make little or no difference, however; what is important is only that whichever rules become established in practice, they be employed by all members of a linguistic community as a necessary means to realizing the shared end.

With the listing of these conditions we would seem to be able to specify the features of conventional comsigns that distinguish them from all other types. To be a proper comsign a sign must satisfy the modified Gricean conditions (1) to (3) of the previous section. To be a conventional comsign it would seem that the use of the sign within a given community must also be a regularity of the kind satisfying conditions (a) to (c).[17] But there is a major difficulty with the added conventionality conditions. Few if any conventions, whether those of etiquette, morals, dress, communication, etc., are ones to which *every* member of a given community conforms or to which everyone expects *all* others to also conform, contrary to conditions (a) and (b). There are invariably some deviations, whether deliberate or inadvertent, and we come to occasionally expect these of at least some others, e.g. the hat worn indoors, the adultery in the neighborhood, the failure to wear a tie at a formal occasion. For linguistic conventions this is obvious in the form of deviations from regularities of syntax and pronunciation. But it also takes the form of deviations from what Ziff terms 'semantic regularities' between types of utterances produced by speakers and states of affairs, e.g. the regularity of correlation between a person's utterances of 'It is raining' and the fact that it is raining, or utterances of 'Red' and the redness of the object pointed to.[18] There will invariably be some instances of the utterances being produced and the states of affairs or property not obtaining. To accommodate these exceptions we could attempt to weaken conditions (a) and (b) by substituting 'nearly everyone usually conforms' for 'everyone conforms'. This would leave us with the problem, however, of specifying how many must conform to the regularity and how often in order for it to be counted as a convention.

No solution to this problem is, of course, possible, and

attempts at arriving at it would miss the essential feature of conventions ignored by Lewis's regularity theory. What marks a convention is not frequency of conformity but how we react to exceptions. It is not simply that our expectations are disappointed and our preferences frustrated. Instead, we react by criticizing an exception as a violation of a rule governing a community practice. An exception is evaluated as 'wrong,' and distinguished from conforming behavior as 'right.' A convention is thus a rule or norm, a standard by which actions are evaluated, not simply the regularity of behavior which results from following a rule. Indoor hat wearers and adulterers may act in irregular and unexpected ways. But it is in virtue of being subject to criticism and their actions judged wrong that conventions are applied to their conduct.[19]

We can attempt to restate conditions necessary for a given sign to be a conventional comsign which incorporate these revisions. A conventional comsign x is one which is a token of a type X governed by a rule R which is such that:

(a') nearly everyone conforms to R in using X;

(b') everyone following R does so with the expectation that nearly everyone else will also conform;

(c') everyone prefers to conform to R on the condition nearly all others do, since R is a solution to a coordination problem P;

(d') violations of R evoke criticisms on the part of others.

It is the addition of (d') that allows us to introduce the qualification 'nearly everyone' in the first two conditions. For sentences as linguistic signs the rules R governing the sign type X are either syntactic, pragmatic, or semantic. Those who mispronounce, fail to have verbs in English agree in number with noun subjects, etc., are open to criticism for failing to observe syntactic rules. Where there is an absence of a conversational implicature, e.g. lack of sincerity when a promise is made or belief when there is an assertion, there is a violation of a pragmatic rule. For violations of semantic rules we employ the term 'false' and contrast them with compliances as what we term 'true'. When it is not raining we judge an utterance of 'It is raining' false. Such a criticism is directed at the speaker for failing to observe conventions necessary for the transmission of information.

It is the applicability of the evaluative terms 'true' and 'false' which principally distinguishes conventional comsigns from the other types of signs so far discussed. We may recall from 3.3 that if on discriminating a natsign the interpreter fails to recognize a significate occurrence at the reference occasion (fails to hear the thunder on seeing the lightning), it is either the significance of events of that type that is changed or in the future events of some other type are discriminated as having the original significance. For non-conventional comsigns recognition of a significate occurrence leads the interpreter I to revise his or her assessment of the communicator C's intentions. Suppose C produces a hissing sound as a transferred natsign, points behind a bush, and I perceive there a goose, not the expected snake. Then I would not apply 'false' to C's sound as a criticism of C, but instead revise his estimate of C's intentions. C will be taken as intending the sound as a sign of a goose, not a snake. Suppose also that C makes an undulating motion which I interprets as an iconic sign of a snake located where C is pointing. If I were to perceive instead a worm, it would again be his interpretation of C's intention that would be revised. The respect by which C intended the gesture to resemble the object pointed to was different from what I had interpreted it to be. As before for the hissing sound, the evaluative term 'false' has no role to play. Similar considerations hold for the application of the evaluative term 'disobey'. Suppose a host makes the palms down seating motion discussed above and the guest does not sit down. Whether we say of him that he disobeyed the gesture hinges on its conventional status. If making the gesture is not for him a rule-governed practice, one which he himself would make in a similar situation, then the criticism has no application. He has simply failed to recognize the host's intention.

This conceptual link between the evaluative terms 'true' and 'false' and the conventionality of a comsign is perhaps the kernel of the correspondence theory of truth, and is emphasized in Austin's defense of it. A statement, he says,

is said to be true when the historic state of affairs to which it is correlated by the demonstrative conventions (the one to which it 'refers') is of a type with which the sentence used in making it is correlated by descriptive conventions.

This correlation, Austin emphasizes, 'is absolutely and purely conventional. We are absolutely free to appoint *any* symbol to *any* type of situation, so far as merely being true goes.'[20] It is only in this sense of a correlation determined by a conventional rule that a statement can be said to 'correspond' to something independent of it. The redundancy or performative theory of truth holds that to judge a comsign 'true' is simply to produce the sign with assertive intent (make a gesture, assert an utterance), or to assent to what is communicated by another. But clearly 'true' has no application where 'false' does not also, and the latter, as we have just seen, has no application to non conventional comsigns. C's hissing sound is a kind of 'assertion', and on seeing a snake behind a bush the interpreter I may assent to the sign, since he or she recognizes what was expected. But since 'false' does not apply to the sound if the expected snake is not there, neither does 'true' if it is. Contrary to the redundancy theory, there may be assertion and assent, and yet no 'truth'.

Do lower animals use conventional comsigns in communicating to one another? S.G. Shanker expresses the view of many when he rejects such a use.[21] Rule-following, he claims, exists only in complex surroundings where there is explanation, correction, and justification that makes reference to the rule, and such activities are language-dependent. Shanker's conclusion is that in the absence of language 'a creature cannot display the degree of complexity which is necesary in order to render regular behavior rule-following behavior.' But this restriction of conventional signs to language-users seems unjustifiably arbitrary. Certainly correction of mistakes is essential for a certain gesture or utterance used within a community to have conventional status. But it is not obvious that such correction must be conducted by linguistic means. It is quite consistent with ethologists' empirical data to suppose a tribe of higher primates, e.g. chimpanzees or gorillas, with distinct utterances for different species of predators. Utterances of type Z might be used to stand for tigers, while Z' stands for boa constrictors. If a sentry posted by the community were to mistakenly utter Z as a warning cry in the presence of a boa constrictor and were subject to later (non-linguistic) correction, perhaps by being attacked by others who repeat Z', then it seems that both Z and Z' would have the status of conventional comsigns. The rules governing the use of both

would be norms governing the signaling practices of that
particular community. Yet the community will lack a communicative system exhibiting all the features of a language.

4.3   Signals

Our focus so far has been on the problems of distinguishing
comsigns from natsigns and of specifying features that serve to
demarcate conventional comsigns. We consider now the internal
structures of comsigns and the logical features of their use and
interpretation. *Complete sentences* are those comsigns with a
subject–predicate structure and whose reference is provided by
subject terms as distinct constituents. The next chapter will be
devoted to these relatively complex comsigns. Here our topic is
comsigns lacking subject–predicate structure, or what we shall
term *signals*. Examples of signals would be the signs of the
previous section – the seating gesture, an animal warning cry, a
hissing sound as a sign of a snake, and a drawing. Included also
would be incomplete single-word sentences such as 'Red', 'Tree',
or 'Mama' of the kind used and interpreted by infants in the early
stages of language acquisition. A complete sentence must
obviously be a conventional sign, with its elements having
conventional meaning and combined by the syntactic rules of a
language. A signal can be either conventional, as for 'Red', or
non-conventional, as for the hissing sound and drawing.

Care must be taken to distinguish our use of the term 'signal'
from that with which it is often employed. Many writers regard
the term as standing for a display, vocalization, or chemical
emission which when produced by a lower animal elicits a reflex
response on the part of others. Thus Sebeok says: 'When a sign
token mechanically or conventionally triggers some reaction on
the part of the receiver, it is said to function as a signal.'[22] For
Hinde the 'message' of a signal is the state of the central nervous
system which causes the signal to be produced; its 'meaning' is
identified with the responses the signal evokes.[23] As has been
emphasized in 3.4, any event which elicits a reflex response is not
a sign as an object of interpretation. It is furthermore not a
proper comsign if not intentionally produced and if recognition of
the communicator's intention is not a reason for the intended
effect being produced. Sebeok and Hinde's signals are thus not

comsigns, and hence not within the extension of the term 'signal' as we are employing the term. As we have emphasized, the extent to which signals function within animal communication is partly an empirical question, partly a decision about extending such terms as 'intend' and 'recognize' to non-human behavioral patterns. The term 'signal' is also used within information theory to refer to the physical medium (e.g. sound wave or light irradiation pattern) by which semantic information is conveyed,[24] while it is taken here to stand for an event as an object of interpretation. Finally, the term is sometimes used for non-linguistic signs formed from a code, e.g. a sequence of dots and dashes of a message in morse code, the semaphore flags of a ship at sea, or the puffs of smoke or drum beats used for communication within primitive societies. But all such encoded signs are interpreted relative to a pre-existing language, and are thus what Morris terms 'post-linguistic' signs.[25] The interpretation of a signal in the sense intended here does not presuppose the capacity to use language.

As a logical term, 'signal' stands for a type of comsign whose reference is not provided by a separate sign constituent. Instead, features of the communication situation and actions of the communicator normally provide this reference and allow an extension of the referent occasion beyond that possible for natsigns. For utterances of single-word sentences such as 'Red' or 'Tree' it is a pointing gesture or perhaps the spatial orientation and eye focus of the speaker that indicate the place at which the hearer is to expect to see the color or object. While for natsigns the spatial location of the referent occasion is contiguous to the occasion at which the sign is perceived, being limited by the associations of past experience, for signals it can be extended to a proximate location that is pointed to or otherwise indicated. Whatever extension there is of the temporal interval between the occasion of sign discrimination and referent occasion is made possible by this extension of location. It is whenever the interpreter goes to the indicated location that he or she is to expect to recognize a significate occurrence.

Signals as objects of dynamic interpretation have accompanying their use the same devices for extending reference. The single-word sentences 'Go' and 'Hit' may again be accompanied by pointing gestures, eye focus, or spatial orientation of speaker indicating the direction in which the action of going is to be performed or at what location there is to be hitting. The indicated direction or location serves to orient the signified action. Non-conventional comsigns such as the hissing sound as a sign of a snake are commonly objects of both cognitive and dynamic interpretation, and for them reference has a dual function. A pointing gesture accompanying the sound would indicate both the location at which the snake could be expected to be seen and from which there should be a retreat. Likewise, the temporal interval within which the snake is to be expected is also that within which the retreat is to be taken.

The single-word sentences mentioned so far, the sentences 'Red', 'Tree', and 'Go', have been formulated with general terms standing for types of features and actions. In its early stages of language acquisition the child learns to interpret and use names such as 'Mama' and 'Daddy' as standing for reidentifiable particular objects. Non-conventional signals seem to be of both general and singular types. The hissing sound can both signify a snake in general or the features of a particular local snake identifiable by both communicator and interpreter; a schematic drawing can be of a tree in general, while a more detailed drawing may be interpreted as standing for aspects unique to a particular tree in the neighborhood. An old man may emit a characteristic wheezing sound as he climbs stairs. Someone A may make this sound and point in a certain direction. Another B familiar with the old man could easily recognize A's intention to alert B of his presence. In such a case B's recognition of a significate occurrence (seeing the old man approach) would in such a case be a reidentification of a particular individual.

We must be careful how we apply the term 'reference' and 'significance' in describing the use and interpretation of singular signals. Suppose an adult were to say 'Mama' to a child learning to speak and point to a certain location. Then the referent of the signal as used on that occasion would be the spatial location indicated by the gesture. It would *not* be the child's mother. In recognizing her mother the child would be recognizing a significate occurrence at the referent occasion, but she would not be identifying the signal's referent. Only for complete sentences which the child will be able later to form, e.g. 'Mama is pretty', will the name have reference as the sentence's subject. Nor should we say that the mother is the signal's significance. The signal token x signifies a complex of features Y as an instance of a type X. It signifies through prior associations between X and Y made when the child learned the name. It is by virtue of these features that the child recognizes at the indicated location her mother. The appearance of those features at this location is the signal's significate occurrence. The recognition of the mother will be that of the same individual seen at previous occasions. But the interpretation of the signal 'Mama' by the child does not seem necessarily to require such recognition of quantitative sameness. It may occur in the early stages of learning that in interpreting the signal the child recognizes only the appearance of Mama-like features without recognizing an individual persisting through time that is reidentified on successive occasions.[26]

Certainly we should not say that the child at this level of language acquisition has the concept of what we call an 'object'. This is a term that is properly applied to the referent of a subject of a complete sentence and only later extended to the referent of 'this' in 'This is pretty' and finally the referent of the implied subject of the single-word sentence 'Pretty'. Of course, in describing the child's interpretation of 'Mama' *we* refer to her recognition of an object at the referent occasion. But if she lacks the capacity to use and interpret a complete sentence in which 'Mama' occurs as subject, the child cannot be said to share our concept. 'Object', like 'quality', 'attribute', and 'relation', stands for a correlate of a sentence-relative logical term. Where no such term is in use it has no application. Recognition of quantitative sameness, in contrast, seems to be a primitive psychological capacity found in lower animals in their reidentification of orienting landmarks and of members of their own species. It is a capacity essential for extended movement, mating, and rearing of offspring, and is present at pre-linguistic stages where the concept of an object is absent.

In Chapter 3 we characterized natsigns as signifying general types of events, and normally this is indeed the case. But even at this level recognition of a significate occurrence can be reidentification. The wheezing sound of the old man may be interpreted by his dog inside the house as a natsign of his master, not simply of someone-in-general. In the direction of the sound the dog may expect the complex of features peculiar to his master, and the sight of him approaching will be the recognition of a significate occurrence. This is also, as for the singular signal, the reidentification of the master as the same individual perceived on prior occasions.

Ronald de Sousa attempts to distinguish human mental capacities from those of sub-human forms by particularity of reference. Sub-human forms of life, he says, exhibit 'quasi-intentionality' when their interpretation of events in their surroundings can be characterized by both intentional inexistence and the generality of what is represented: 'the "object" represented will always remain a *general type*, never a particular.' In contrast, full-fledged intentionality requires both intentional inexistence and 'the capacity for singular reference' to material particulars.[27] Intentional inexistence is present, of course, in all sign interpretation, since there may be a significate non-occurrence at the referent occasion. Singular reference, in contrast, is present only for subject–predicate sentences for which, as De Sousa notes, it is possible that there be substitution of co-referring singular terms. His quasi-intentionality thus characterizes the interpretation of natsigns and signals, while intentionality characterizes the peculiarly human interpretation of sentences. The reference of natsigns and signals is to a time and place, not to a reidentifiable object. But this should not be understood as denying of sub-human forms the capacity for recognizing an individual as what has been previously experienced. The significance of all signs is a general type of event, but for some primitive signs recognition of a significate occurrence seems to be also recognition of quantitative sameness.

Besides the introduction of supplementing devices for extending reference, the communicative context of signals serves to introduce two additional features not present at the level of natsigns. The first is the presence of a means by which the communicator can convey how a given signal is intended to be understood by its interpreter, or its *illocutionary force*. Here it is communicated primarily by varying the intonation, volume, or frequency of a vocalization. Thus, the degree of urgency of an animal warning cry can be indicated by its loudness or the frequency with which it is repeated. A single-word imperative such as 'Go' can be uttered with variations in intonation which indicate whether it is intended as a command or request. In such cases the force of an utterance is what the speaker intends it to have, provided the interpreter recognizes the intention, with intonation being the device by which this intention is expressed. Illocutionary force indicators can be conventionalized; as we shall see in the next chapter, separate linguistic expressions can take on this role. But even here they are primarily expressive of the purposes to which the communicator intends a comsign to be put, different in this respect from conventional comsigns like 'Red' or 'Tree' whose significance is independent from the intentions with which they may be produced.

The second feature added at the level of signals is a means by which we are enabled to determine both the source of a signal and its intended interpreter or audience. In face-to-face communication where there is visual contact, the signal's source is primarily indicated to the interpreter simply by his or her observing the communicator's movements and for a verbal utterance perhaps also recognizing the direction from which a sound is emitted. In such situations orientation of the communicator and eye focus are usually the primary means for indicating the intended target or addressee. Such devices for indicating both the source and target we shall refer to as the *addresses* of the signal.

For relatively long-distance communication with no visual contact addresses take other forms. Individual differences in sound patterns often enable a hearer to recognize a signal's source, as when we recognize the voice of a friend over the phone. Ethologists have noted features of sounds emitted by lower animals which function as 'signatures' identifying their individual sources. These signatures can also provide more general information, identifying the sex of the source, much as voice pitch distinguishes males from females for humans, or identifying the species of the communicator and even the local interbreeding population to which it belongs, as may occur for mating and territorial bird calls.[28] Assuming these are indeed signals as comsigns and not 'social releasers' triggering reflex responses, these signatures would be source addresses indicating either the identity of the source or more general information about it. Target addresses at the level of signals seem less common for long-distance communication. A signal itself can sometimes function to alert the intended addressee. If the child shouts 'Mama!', she may be intending to elicit a helping response. But she will also be indicating from whom this response is to come. As we readily see from this account, addresses exist only in primitive forms at the level of signals. With language and cultural institutions providing the context for its use they begin to take on more detailed and effective forms. The discussion of this we postpone until Section 5.4 in the next chapter.

4.4   Features of communicative systems

By a *communicative system* is simply meant a set of significant sign elements used to communicate between members of a community. A human language is such a system with certain unique features. Signaling systems found used by sub-human species seems to exhibit some of these features as a matter of contingent fact, and empirical studies of animal communication have sought to determine the particular combinations of features present for given species. A central goal of philosophical semiotic is, in contrast, to specify what features are *possible* at the level of signals and which ones are *necessary* and to contrast them to features that are necessary for language. A review of the principal features of language is essential for an attempt at this task. There are altogether six of them that are important for our purposes.[29]

1 *Semanticity*. This feature is present when the elements of the system are objects of cognitive interpretation and are related by interpreters to independent events or things in the environment. Single-word imperatives such as 'Go' or 'Run' have semanticity, since their verbs can also be used to describe actions of others, as in 'Goes' or 'Runs'. But it is conceivable that there be communicative systems whose elements are only used to prescribe and which would thus lack this feature. Ethologists note how many animal signals seem to have only an expressive or addressing function, the information they convey being about the state of the communicator, not independent environmental events. Bird calls, for example, seem usually to have the addressing function of announcing the presence of the caller for such purposes as mating or territorial defense. At other times

they are used for expressing alarm. For young chicks a cry is expressive of hunger. For all such cases semanticity would be absent.

2 *Conventionality*. The conditions for conventionality have been discussed in 4.2 and need not be repeated. It is marked by the arbitrariness of the elements of a communicative system, as contrasted with elements bearing an iconic relation to what they signify. Whether this feature presupposes semanticity is a difficult question. It might seem possible for a set of conventional elements to be used solely for prescriptive purposes and be objects of dynamic interpretation only, and thus lack semanticity. But it is difficult to conceive how the significance of such elements could be learned by an interpreter. Learning would seem to require a correlation between elements and independent things or events, as when we teach the child the meaning of 'Runs' by pointing to running people and only afterwards expect her to obey the command 'Run' by imitating what she has previously observed. The situation seems the same for expressions of emotions or feelings. The child learns at some stage to control her spontaneous cries, and the cry then becomes a non-conventional comsign used to express pain or discomfort and solicit attention. But such conventional signs as 'Hurts' or 'Ouch' seem to be used in their place only after the child has learned to associate them with the behavior of others. Conventionality thus does seem to pre-suppose semanticity.

3 *Semantic field placement*. This is our term for relationships which elements of a communicative system can bear to each other. It occurs when a given number of mutually exclusive elements together exhaust a semantic field, as for the list of color adjectives 'red', 'orange', 'yellow', 'blue', etc. which exhaust the semantic field of color and for which no two such predicates can be jointly predicated at a given location. The meaning of a color adjective, e.g. 'orange', is determined by its position relative to other words such as 'red' and 'yellow' to the extent that one who knows this position would seem to be able to understand the meaning of 'orange' without having had prior experience of the color (Hume's idea without a corresponding impression). By adding a color adjective, say 'pink', which serves to partition the field for more precise discriminations, the meanings of 'neighboring' words such as 'red' are altered. Similar considerations hold

for action verbs such as 'run', 'walk', 'crawl', 'hop', etc. which exhaust the semantic field of self-locomotive movement. Introducing another word such as 'trot' has again the effect of altering the other words such as 'run'. Where a list of n elements X_1, X_2, . . . , X_n exhaust a semantic field an interpreter I expects at a given referent occasion to recognize an occurrence of the significance of either X_1 or of X_2 . . . or of X_n. If a communicator signals a token of X_1, then if a significate non-occurrence is recognized I would perceive an occurrence of one of the other X_2, X_3, . . . ,X_n. Thus, on hearing 'Red' accompanied by a pointing gesture a hearer on not seeing red would expect to see at the indicated location either orange or yellow or blue, etc. It seems obvious that semantic field placement is a feature which requires the conventionality of the communicative system. How many elements exhaust a given semantic field and hence their significance can vary from one speech community to another, depending on the purposes of the community in which the system is functioning.

4 *Duality of patterning.* Let X_1, . . . ,X_n now be a list of the *basic elements* of a communicative system, those minimal significant elements which cannot be analyzed into other sign elements having significance. A *complex signal* is a signal formed by combining two or more of these basic elements, in contrast to a basic element used in isolation as a *simple signal.* The basic elements of a spoken human language are its morphemes. For English they are the sounds corresponding to such inscriptions as 'big', 'dig', 'ly', 'boy', 'toy', and 's'. Those which can be used in isolation to communicate, e.g. 'big', 'dig', 'boy', and 'toy', are the linguist's 'free' morphemes; those which can occur only in combination with others, e.g. 'ly' by which adverbial modification is indicated or 's' indicating the plural of nouns, are the 'bound' morphemes of a given language. Patterned combinations of morphemes without subject–predicate structure such as 'big toy' would thus constitute complex signals formed from the basic elements of the English linguistic communicative system. More generally, a complex signal is some combination $X_1 + X_2 + . . . + X_n$ of n basic elements X_1, X_2, . . . ,X_n where $n > 1$.[30]

Human languages also have a second level of patterning by which their basic elements are formed by combinations of phonemes as *sub-elements* which themselves lack significance.

Phonemes correspond roughly to a language's vowels and consonants, and are the contrastive sounds which function to distinguish one morpheme from another. Thus, the sounds corresponding to 'b' and 'd' are phonemes, for they function to distinguish 'big' from 'dig' as distinct morphemes with different meanings. This second level of patterning enables the generation of a potentially infinite number of morphemes by combinations and reiterations of a relatively small number of sub-elements.

Human languages exhibit this duality of patterning, and they seem to be unique in this respect.[31] But it is at least possible that more primitive signaling systems exhibit this feature as well. The first level of patterning is clearly independent of the conventionality feature, as a communicator could combine iconic gestures to form a complex signal. This level may also not require semanticity, since gestures used solely to prescribe actions would also seem capable of combination. But since the second level requires discrete sub-elements, in contrast to those that vary continuously over such ranges as pitch and intensity, it would seem to require the conventionality of the basic elements formed from them, and hence also the first and second features that conventionality presupposes. Both levels of patterning would seem to be independent of semantic field placement, since basic elements need not bear any field-dependent relationships to one another.

5 *Grammaticality*. Suppose $X_1 + X_2$ to be a complex signal composed of two basic elements X_1 and X_2. If the order between these elements is relevant to the meaning of the whole, that is if $X_1 + X_2$ has a different meaning for an interpreter than does $X_2 + X_1$, we shall say that the system in which the signal is formed exhibits *weak grammaticality*. Systems will also exhibit this feature if they have rules specifying how the form of one element is to depend on the form of the other, as the form of an adjective in French or Latin may be determined by the gender of the noun it modifies. Suppose now a complex comsign to have two significant elements (not necessarily basic) X_s and X_p, with X_s having a referring function and X_p being used to describe the object referred to by X_s. Then we have a *sentence* governed by rules indicating the differing functions of X_s and X_p. These elements may be conventional, as for 'Apple, red' said by a child

just beginning to learn to combine words into sentences. But we can also conceive of a combination of two iconic gestures, one referring to an object and the other representing an attribute or action to be performed on it. Thus, a person could make an undulating motion representing a snake and then a hitting gesture intended to convey to another that he is to hit the snake. Any such complex comsign will be governed by rules for combining X_s and X_p, possibly only ordering rules indicating their different functions. For human languages the rules include those for agreement between nouns and verbs. A communicative system with weak grammaticality and also rules for these subject–predicate combinations we shall say exhibits *strong grammaticality*.[32] The rules are conventional (though the elements to which they are applied may not be), and hence grammaticality, both weak and strong, requires conventionality. Strong grammaticality requires also semanticity, since a subject element or term X_s must refer to an object in the environment of communicator and interpreter. Strong grammaticality is obviously a special kind of first-level patterning, but does not require the combined elements X_s and X_p to be formed by second-level patterning.

6 *Displacement*. Displacement occurs when a communicator uses a comsign which refers the interpreter to a referent occasion remote in time and space from the occasion at which the sign occurs. The primary means for making this possible is the use of sentences with subject–predicate structure. Use of a subject term as a distinct constituent enables a speaker to refer to a distant object which the hearer can identify. The referent occasion then becomes the indefinite occasion at which the object referred to is identified. To say 'Fire' along with a pointing gesture allows reference only to a place in the vicinity of the speaker and hearer. But to say 'Morris Library is on fire' allows the speaker to refer to a building which may be miles or even hundreds of miles distant. The referent occasion is the place at which the hearer would identify a building as referred to by the subject 'Morris Library'. It might be thought that displacement could be accomplished by other means. We can imagine a person saying 'Fire' and pointing in a certain direction with a rotating movement, with each complete arm rotation indicating a certain interval of distance, say 500 yards. Then three rotations would

indicate a fire at a distance of almost a mile, a remote location indeed. But to teach someone how to interpret such a gesture would seem to require a prior ability to use language and formulate subject–predicate sentences. We certainly would not expect a dog or chimpanzee to be able to hear 'Fetch' accompanied by a rotating gesture and be able to fetch a distant object in response to it. The waggle dance of honey bee scouts indicates by orientation and frequency the direction and distance of sources of honey, and the distance can measure several hundred feet.[33] But this seems to be an evolved pattern of behavior which is innate and only triggers reflex responses in other bees. Since it is not an object of interpretation, it cannot be compared to the functioning of a subject of a sentence.

If displacement is a feature present only at the level of sentences with subject–predicate structure, then it is clearly accompanied by strong grammaticality and the features grammaticality presupposes. Whether conventionality is also required is less clear. It might seem that the iconic gesture representing a snake could refer to a distant reptile familiar to both communicator and interpreter. But the likelihood of misinterpreting the gesture seems greater the more remote the referent. Is it the large or small snake? Or could it be a goose both are familiar with? Iconic subjects seem to have at best an incidental, occasional use. In practice it seems they will invariably become conventionalized as a means of insuring that the interpreter identify what the communicator intends.

Having outlined these six features, we are in a position to give an abstract characterization of a language. A *language* can be defined as a communicative system with duality of patterning, displacement, and strong grammaticality. These features entail, as we have seen, conventionality and hence also semanticity. Actual human languages possess also the feature of semantic field placement, making possible along with the other features unlimited expressibility, the capacity of language users to form an unlimited number of complex combinations of basic elements and to express more precisely intended meanings by introducing more elements to exhaust a given semantic field. The size of an object can be initially described by 'big', 'small', 'large', and 'short', and then later by measurements such as '8 cubic feet', '2.6

centimeters', '4.76301 millimeters', etc. Each new system of elements introduced to exhaust the semantic field of size enables finer discriminations between objects.

Of the features essential to a language displacement and strong grammaticality accompanying subject–predicate structure seems most central. We can conceive of signaling systems lacking these features but possessing all or some of the remaining ones. In particular, it seems possible for a system to have semanticity, conventionality, semantic field placement, duality of patterning, and weak grammaticality, and hence give its users the capacity to form an unlimited number of complex signals by which environmental objects and events could be discriminated. In fact, ethologists have tentatively concluded that none or at most one or two of these features are found in actual signaling systems used in communities of lower animals. Why is this so? The answer seems to be that the conveying of the increased information made possible by such features has little use in the absence of displacement. Without displacement, signal users are alerting others to proximate things and events, and for this a limited number of signals standing for food sources or predators, identifying members of the community, and directing a few distinct actions are sufficient. Once the displacement enabled by the subject–predicate structure of sentences was achieved, man could anticipate and react to what was remote in time and space. Also, as we shall see in the next chapter, subject terms could become what we can term 'condensation points' for the accumulation of stored information. Displacement requires, in turn, more precise descriptions and specifications of ways of satisfying wants. For this the other features characteristic of human languages are required.

The humanistic tradition that followed Descartes has located the 'Great Divide' between man and other animal species in a metaphysical distinction. Man has mentality characterized by cognition and free will; lower animals are machines with perhaps traces of accompanying sensations and feelings. Linguistic signs are for man objects of consciousness; animal signals are stimuli triggering reflex responses. As we become more aware of the complexity of behavior of all animals the basis for this distinction seems less plausible. It is more likely that the Great Divide is located in the form of sign which we have the unique capacity to use and interpret, the sentence with subject–predicate structure by which reference to the remote is made possible. There seem to be no justifiable reasons for not extending whatever metaphysical views we may form of this form of sign interpretation to the interpretation of signs at all levels.

We turn now to an examination of the use of sentences, a task that has been a major preoccupation of philosophy for most of this century. Unlike much of this recent tradition, however, our attention will be on features of sentences that compare and contrast them with the signs discussed in this and the previous chapter.

# 5 LANGUAGE

We now return to where we began, to the language used in daily conversation with which we are most familiar. But in matters philosophical familiarity breeds misunderstanding. Having set forth the basic features of more primitive signs we should be in a better position now to isolate those features of linguistic signs which compare and contrast them to the lower-level signs of the previous two chapters. We begin in the first section by outlining some basic and much-discussed features of subject–predicate sentences, and then discuss expressions which are intermediate between them and signals. The next three sections focus on controversial topics in the philosophy of language: the relation between a sentence's subject term and its referent, the relation between the meaning of a sentence and both the truth and illocutionary force of an utterance of it, and the functions of the first and second person pronouns 'I' and 'you'. We shall see how the perspective offered by semiotic enables a clarification of problems in these three areas and indicates clues to their solution. Finally, in the last section we sketch some of the special features introduced when sentences occur within discourse contexts.

5.1 The role of subjects

A language is, as we have just seen in the previous section, a communicative system with a lexicon consisting of a finite number of morphemes as basic elements and grammatical rules for combining these morphemes to form subject–predicate sentences and combinations of such sentences. As linguists often stress, the word is a derivative element, a special kind of morpheme or combination of morphemes which takes on importance when writing develops as a means of preserving speech and enabling long-distance communication. Following

Morris we can define a *lansign* as any combination of morphemes capable of performing a communicative function, whether that of conveying information, prescribing actions, reporting sensations, expressing feelings or emotions, etc. A lansign is either a sentence or a discourse as a combination of sentences about some common topic, e.g. a narrative, inference, or directive.[1]

Sentences as basic lansigns can be analyzed into *terms* as their logical elements. A term can be defined as a morpheme or combination of morphemes with a distinct logical function, whether that of being used to refer to an object or objects, ascribing an attribute or relation, or (in the case of imperatives) prescribing an action. A sentence's *subject terms* or *subjects* have the referring function, its *predicate* the ascribing or prescribing. As is often emphasized by logicians, the category of logical subject does not necessarily coincide with the category of grammatical subject. In 'John is tall' 'John' is both the grammatical and logical subject. But in the relational sentence 'John hit Bill' both 'John' and 'Bill' are classified as logical subjects, though only the former is a grammatical one. The logical classification is due to both names performing the same referring role. Within a given term it is also useful to distinguish what we can term its *nucleus*, the word which is central to it, and other words, phrases, or clauses which function to qualify or modify it, the *qualifiers* of the nucleus. Within subjects a noun is invariably the nucleus; in predicates this role can be assumed by an adjective or verb as well as a noun. Thus, in the sentence 'The tall man who was whistling walked quickly down the street' 'man' is the nucleus of the definite description which serves as the sentence's singular subject, while 'tall' and the relative clause 'who was whistling' are its qualifiers. In the predicate the verb 'walked' is the nucleus, while the adverb 'quickly' and the prepositional phrase 'down the street' are its qualifiers.[2] How nuclei and qualifiers are combined to form terms and terms combined to form sentences will vary according to the syntactic rules unique to a given language.

Our examples so far have been of *singular sentences*, sentences whose subjects are used to refer to individual objects. *General sentences* are those whose subjects are general terms used to refer to a plurality of objects, sentences such as 'Few cats swim', 'Most dogs bark', 'All men are mortal', 'Some men are wise', etc. In such sentences the expressions 'few', 'most', 'all', and 'some' function as *quantifiers*, indicating how many there are of the objects referred to by the general subjects 'cats', 'dogs', and 'men' to which the predicates are being ascribed.

At the level of subject–predicate sentences, whether singular or general, two important features appear which are not present for either natsigns or signals. These are explained as follows.

Referent occasion extension. In the last two chapters we have seen how limited in time and space is the referent occasion of a token of a natsign and signal. In contrast, for sentences the referent occasion becomes whenever and wherever the interpreter identifies the object or objects referred to by the subject. This identification requires either prior acquaintance with these objects or previous information about them. Recognition of a significate occurrence or non-occurrence at the referent occasion we term at this level a 'judgment' of truth or falsity or an 'assent' or 'denial' to an utterance of the sentence (or in the more usual terminology the 'statement' the sentence is being used to make). Instead of the more general term 'expectation' applied at the lower levels of interpretation, it is more customary to describe the psychological state aroused by an utterance of a sentence as one of 'belief.'

This extension of reference is both spatial and temporal. For a token of a signal the referent occasion is determined, as we saw in 4.3, by the context in which it is produced and limited in spatial extent to proximate locations that can be indicated by gestures or the communicator's orientation. For sentence tokens, in contrast, the referent occasion can be as remote as the objects which are later identified as their referents.[3] It is anywhere that John can be located that can serve as an occasion for judging an utterance of 'John is tall' true or false. Limits to the temporal interval within which this identification can take place are set by the context of utterance and the tense of the sentence.[4] 'John is sitting' would not be judged false if John were to later stand at some occasion subsequent to the occasion of utterance. While the referent occasion for natsigns and signals seems limited to what is contemporaneous or in the near future of the sign token, for sentence tokens this occasion can lie in the past as indicated by a past tense form of the verb. For a sentence such as 'John was sitting' the information conveyed seems equivalent to a counter-factual conditional stating that if the hearer had identified the referent John at some past time *t* he would have recognized John to be sitting at *t*. Verbal indicators of spatial location can be included within the subject term. We say 'This man is sitting' or 'That book over there is red', indicating with the demonstratives 'this', 'that', and 'there' the location of the man or book to which the attributes are being ascribed. The temporal position of an object is, in fact, determined by verb tense. But it seems an accidental grammatical feature of languages that places temporal indicators within the predicate and not, as for demonstratives, within the subject. Logically tense does seem to belong with the subject, indicating when the subject's referent must be identified for the predicate to be expected to hold of it.[5]

Subject terms within imperatives perform a role similar to that in the indicative sentences we have been discussing. In sentences such as 'Kick the ball' or 'Go to the store' the singular subjects 'the ball' and 'the store' refer to objects whose identification serves to orient the action being commanded. Gestures accompanying the single-word commands 'Kick' and 'Go' can indicate the place at which the kicking is to be performed or the direction of going, but both will be tied to the immediate environment in a way not necessary when the subjects are added. The object referred to by a singular subject will be typically perceptually identified in the process of obeying an utterance of an imperative. In contrast, we usually assent to or accept as true an utterance of an indicative without actual perceptual identification, relying instead on prior acquaintance or background information to identify the referent and basing our assent on a belief in the speaker's reliability. This acceptance without judgment constitutes a type of partial interpretation (cf. 3.3). Someone says to me 'A truck has overturned and blocked the highway'. I respond by taking the exit and making a detour, thus avoiding a delay. Extension of the referent occasion in such cases enables interpreters to avoid perceptual identification of a referent distant in space which is associated with a potential harm.

Information transfer and storage. The second feature distinguishing sentences from signals is related to the first. Let S be a singular subject and P a predicate that are combined to form the sentence S/P. If an interpreter I accepts S/P as true or assents to it, then the information expressed by the predicate P will tend to be transferred to the subject S and used on some future occasion to identify the object it is being used to refer to. Thus, if our subject is the descriptive phrase 'the man' within the sentence 'The man is old' which is accepted as true, then in the future 'the old man' will tend to be used to identify its referent. The sentence 'The man is sitting' would be interpreted as saying 'The old man is sitting'. If this is accepted as true, then the phrase 'the old man who is sitting' will be used to identify, and the sentence 'The man is tired' becomes interpreted as 'The old man who is sitting is tired'. And similarly for the predicate 'is tired' if an utterance of this last sentence is accepted. More generally, let S/P_1, S/P_2, . . . ,S/P_n be n number of sentences which are accepted as true, and let P_{n+1} be a predicate ascribing a further attribute to the individual referred to by S. Then S/P_{n+1} will tend to be interpreted as $S+P_1+P_2+ . . . +P_n/P_{n+1}$, with $S+P_1+P_2+ . . . +P_n$ a complex descriptive phrase consisting of a nucleus S plus n number of qualifiers $P_1,P_2, . . . ,P_n$ derived from what were originally predicates. Subject terms are thus to be regarded as what we can metaphorically term 'accumulation points' for the 'storage' of information conveyed by predicates of sentences previously accepted as true. This accumulation process can continue for an indefinite number of predicates. In this way answers to the question 'Which S?' ('Which man?') are given, and identification of referent is increasingly freed from the need for indexical devices such as context, orientation, and gestures.[6] When S occurs as a subject of an imperative such as 'Go to the man', actions can also now be prescribed with less reliance on these devices.

When proper names occur as singular subjects a similar transference occurs. If a person were to successively assent to 'John is a man', 'John is old', and 'John lives next door', the information conveyed by 'man', 'old', and 'lives next door' would be transferred to the subject 'John' and used in the future as criteria for identifying an individual as its referent. Someone assenting to these three sentences could substitute for the proper name the definite description 'the old man who lives next door' with 'man' as nucleus on hearing a future occurence of the name. Thus, he would interpret the sentence 'John is tired' as meaning

'The old man who lives next door is tired'. More generally, on assenting to n sentences S/P_1, S/P_2, . . . ,S/P_n, a person can substitute for the name S the combination P_1+P_2+ . . . $+P_n$ in the form of a definite description. A new sentence S/P_{n+1} then becomes interpreted as P_1+P_2+ . . . $+P_n/P_{n+1}$. Though the interpreter may not be able to formulate explicitly the definite description that is to be substituted, he will usually be able to use the attributes expressed by $P_1,P_2,$ . . . ,P_n as criteria for identifying an individual as the referent of S.

We noted in Section 4.2 the contrast between conventional signals and natsigns with respect to the effect of recognition of a significate non-occurrence on the sign's significance. For natsigns such recognition can lead to a change of significance, while to judge a conventional signal as 'false' leads to no change, though it can bring about a change in the assessment of the communicator's reliability. At the level of sentences this contrast becomes more complicated. Assent or dissent to an utterance of a sentence does not affect the meaning of its predicate; this part of the sentence is similar in this respect to a signal. But we have just seen how assent to or acceptance of an utterance can change the meaning of the sentence's subject, causing a transference to it of information conveyed by the predicate and changing the criteria for identification of referent that is later used. For dissent or denial there is normally no change in the subject's meaning, but instead, as for conventional signals, a reassessment of the speaker's reliability. In certain circumstances, however, change in the subject's meaning can also occur where an utterance is judged false. Suppose the interpreter I accepts 'John is a man' and 'John is old' as true at time t_1 and that later at t_2 uses the description 'The old man' to identify the referent of 'John is sitting'. Suppose also that I judges an utterance of this latter sentence conveyed by a speaker as false. Then the speaker could be assessed as unreliable. But it may be that I identified as John the wrong individual on the basis of an error in the utterance accepted at t_1. John may not have been old, though I believed he was, as age was used as a criterion in his mistaken identification of the referent of 'John' at t_2. Then the denial at t_2 may be itself mistaken: John *is* sitting, though the individual I takes to be John may not be. If the interpreter I were to realize this mistake, the effect of the correction would be to change the meaning of 'John' for him: the attribute of being old is no longer used as a criterion for identification. As we shall see in the next section, the possibility of misinformation being transferred to the subject is sufficient to refute one of the leading theories of proper names.[7]

So far we have discussed only singular subject–predicate sentences, with speech the mode of communication between communicator and interpreter. Of the many other varieties of sentences those indicatives lacking logical subjects and intermediate between signals and complete sentences are of special interest. These are what, following Strawson, we term *feature-placing sentences*, sentences used to describe a feature without reference to a reidentifiable object. Examples of these are 'It is raining' and sentences such as 'There is gold here' and 'Here is some water' in which the mass nouns 'gold' and 'water' occur. The sentence 'It is raining' has the pronoun 'it' as a grammatical subject, but it is clearly not used to refer. It is rather a grammatical device added to conform to the general requirement for a subject.[8] It is just as obvious that in 'There is gold here' the word 'there' is not a logical subject enabling identification. To judge an utterance of a feature-placing sentence true is to recognize at a referent occasion indicated by context and verb tense the type of feature signified by verb forms such as 'raining' or mass nouns such as 'gold' and 'water'. Lacking a subject term, there is no object identified as quantitatively the same as one encountered in previous experience. Interpretation thus exhibits the same basic features as are present for signals, even though the syntactic form of a sentence is exhibited.

Quine speculates that for infants a name such as 'Mama' initially functions as a means of recognizing a recurring feature in their environment. It is only at a later stage that the name is applied to an individual reidentified as quantitatively the same on successive occasions.[9] Similar considerations would seem hold for nouns such as 'cat' and 'tree', which may be initially interpreted as mass nouns standing for cat-like or tree-like features. Later when criteria for identifying an object as the same cat or the same tree become associated with them they, like proper names, can function as logical subjects.[10] The transition is thus from using 'Mama', 'Cat', and 'Tree' as single-word feature-placing sentences having the logical features of signals, to using them as the subjects of complete sentences.

Also of importance for our comparative purposes are comsigns not formed from the lexicon of a language in accordance with its grammatical rules, but having sentence-like features. Among these are signs whose 'predicates' are iconic representations and whose 'subjects' are singular or general terms referring to the object or objects to which the representation is to be applied. A portrait with the name of the individual portrayed under it is just such a sentence-like icon, as would be a landscape painting with the name of the place as caption or title.[11] For both the names function to identify for the viewer the individual or place represented. Other examples would include a map with place names included and a circuit diagram with a caption or title indicating the product being diagrammed. In Section 3.2 we excluded photographs along with TV images from the class of natsigns, arguing that they were instead ways of perceiving objects. Adding the names of individuals photographed or an announcer's voice identifying what is being depicted on the screen would not seem to force a revision of this exclusion. The names or the announcer's description simply identify for the viewer what he is looking at by means of the photographs or screen images, much as a tourist guide labels buildings and places for us as we view them on tours. There is thus a fundamental contrast between an intentionally produced painting, map, or diagram as an iconic comsign and a photograph or screen image as related causally to what it is a means of perceiving.

5.2 Denotation and reference

In Section 1.1 we saw how in evaluating inferences we must assume that different occurrences of the same singular term refer to the same individual. Without this assumption not even the most basic of inferences, 'John is sitting; therefore, John is sitting', could be evaluated as valid, since the occurrence of 'John' in the conclusion might be used to refer to an individual different from that referred to by the same name in the premiss. In this way logic can ignore the relations of a subject term to its user and the occasion of use and stipulate a dyadic relation between the term and its object. This relation is said to be that of *denotation* (sometimes *designation*) and the unique object denoted by a singular term is called its *denotatum*. A given singular term S is said to denote an individual object if and only if S is true of this object. Thus, the name 'John' denotes (or designates) a given individual if and only if 'John' can be truly ascribed of this individual. Similarly, a general subject such as 'cats' is said to denote the class of objects, its *denotata*, to which it can be truly ascribed, i.e. the class of cats.

For terms occurring within inferential contexts it may be possible to abstract such a denotation relation. But outside of such contexts and for terms used as the subjects of sentences conveying information or prescribing actions no such relation exists. Instead, within such sentences a singular subject is used by a person on a given occasion to refer to an object. What is termed *reference* is a triadic relation between an utterance of a sentence as used by a person at a certain time and place, and this relation has very different features from the dyadic relation postulated in logical evaluation.[12] The difference can be seen most clearly by examining attempts to specify the dyadic denotation relation for a singular subject of a sentence isolated from an inferential context. For such a relation we can ask of a given singular subject what the unique object is that it denotes. Two theories have been proposed to answer this question for proper names.

The first is the so-called 'Description Theory' of names originally proposed by Frege. Every proper name, the theory claims, expresses a number of attributes by virtue of which a given individual can be identified as its denotatum. These attributes can be expressed by a definite description which can be substituted for the name, as we can substitute for 'Aristotle' the definite description 'The author of *Prior Analytics* and teacher of Alexander the Great'. According to the description theory the denotatum of the name is the individual of which this substituted description is true. Thus, the name 'Aristotle' denotes the individual to which we can truly ascribe the attributes of being the author of *Prior Analytics* and teacher of Alexander the Great.

It should be clear from what was said about meaning transference from predicates to subjects in the previous section why this theory is mistaken. As we saw, when utterances of singular sentences S/P_1 and S/P_2 have been accepted as true, we tend to employ P_1+P_2 as a definite description for purposes of identification and substitute it for S in a third sentence S/P_3. If this is how names acquire meaning, then obviously the substituted description can be false of the object we take it to denote or designate. For though we may have accepted sentences S/P_1 and S/P_2 as true, they may in fact prove to be false. In that case the description P_1+P_2 would be false of the object we take as the denotatum of S. Thus, we may have accepted as true that Aristotle is the author of *Prior Analytics* and teacher of Alexander, but one or both attributes we may learn later do not apply. Then 'Aristotle' would not denote the individual having these attributes, though they may be expressed by the name as currently used by us. John Searle has attempted a modification of the description theory to account for this difficulty. A name may express a number of attributes and a given definite description will be a selection from amongst this total set. There will then be a range of alternative descriptions $D_1, D_2, \ldots, D_n$ which we may employ as substitutes for the name. Any one attribute or even several attributes that we take the name to express as the result of transference may be false of the denoted object. But Searle contends that a certain sub-set or cluster of these attributes must hold of the object in order for it to be the denotatum, and thus the disjunction D_1 or $D_2 \ldots$ or D_n must be true of it.[13]

As Kripke points out, however, it is possible to conceive of cases where not even this weakened condition holds.[14] It is possible, for example, that all we have accepted of the individual called 'Aristotle' – his authorship of philosophical writings, study at Plato's Academy, instruction of Alexander, etc. – is revealed false by later scholarship. It is not Aristotle who can be described in this way, but some other individual, much as some would have Bacon as the author of the plays now attributed to the man we call 'Shakespeare'. In such a case none of the alternative descriptions we substitute for the name is true of the denoted individual, and hence Searle's modified description theory is false.

As an alternative Kripke and others propose what is labelled the 'causal theory' of denotation. According to it a proper name denotes that individual to which the name is causally related. For a historical figure a name is initially bestowed directly by a process of labelling or baptism. The name's denotatum is this initially labelled object, with a process of historical transmission providing the causal link to the present. Thus, the name 'Aristotle' denotes the individual so named about 300 BC, an individual who may in fact have none of the attributes we currently believe him to have and associate with the name. The causal relation between the initially named individual and the name in current use is maintained as the name is continued in use through successive generations.[15]

Such a theory can easily be shown to be false of names as they occur in the context of sentences used in ordinary conversation. In the first place it is rare that a given name is bestowed on a unique individual. Almost invariably a name will be bestowed on several, as witnessed by the many occurrences of a name such as 'John Smith' in the phone book. But then there will be several alternative routes of historical transmission from individual baptisms to a present use of the name, and the theory itself proposes no criterion for selecting between them. I can use the name 'Aristotle' intending to refer to Aristotle Onassis, not an individual born about 300 BC. The causal theory has no means of determining that it is in fact the late husband of Jacqueline Onassis I am referring to and not the historical figure. Second, there are many occasions where we refer to an individual by a name which is not his and was never bestowed on him. I may mistakenly call an individual named 'John' by the name 'Peter' or jokingly refer to a certain contemporary philosopher as 'Aristotle'. Provided my audience recognizes whom I am intending to refer to, the referents of 'Peter' and 'Aristotle' as used by me then are not the individuals originally baptized with these names, but instead John and the living philospher. Hence, what is claimed to be the denotatum of the name by the causal theory is not its referent as used by me on that occasion.

The common mistake of both the description and causal theories can be traced to their assumption that it makes sense to attempt to determine the unique subject denoted by a name within the context of an isolated sentence. Names within such contexts, as contrasted to those occurring in sentences within inferential contexts, are used by speakers to refer to objects, and this reference is successful if the hearer is able to identify the same object to which the speaker intends to refer. It is nonsense to ask what such a name denotes, since it is not possible to abstract a denotation relation within such a context. Instead, we must ask what the speaker intends the name to refer to and whether the hearer is able to identify the intended referent, a referent which will vary with the occasion of use. The intended referent may not satisfy a given definite description, whether itself used as the singular subject or substituted on the basis of meaning transference for a proper name. I may say to another 'The bald man over there is tired' when in fact the man I indicate and believe is bald is not bald. As long as the hearer is able to identify the referent I intend, reference has been successful, a success that may be due either to the hearer sharing my mistaken belief, to my realizing that he holds the belief and choosing the description in order to guide him, or to his realizing my belief and thereby identifying the referent. We saw above in Section 4.2 how Grice's attempt to equate the meaning of a comsign with what a speaker intends it to mean on a given occasion fails for conventional signs. But it does seem that we can equate the referent of a given subject term with what the speaker intends it to refer to on a given occasion, provided he or she has provided reasonable means for the hearer to identify this intended referent.[16]

The description theory gains its plausibility from the function of the subject term to extend reference. Where the intended referent is in the immediate vicinity and the speaker knows well the beliefs of a specific audience the speaker can employ what he knows is a false description. But for distant objects and for an indefinite audience the speaker will employ what he believes is a true description and what is commonly accepted as true within the wider community of which he is a part. Only in this way can he have assurance that reference will be successful, that what he intends to refer to will be identified. The acceptance of the description as true within the community does not, of course, guarantee that it will not be later rejected as false on the basis of further evidence. But this later rejection in no way affects the present usefulness of the term in enabling the audience to identify what is intended. It is in fact misleading to speak of subject terms, whether names or descriptions, as being true or false. It is utterances of sentences which are judged true or false, and this occurs when their predicates express types of features recognized as true of the referents of their subjects. The subjects are efficacious or not in enabling identification of these referents, but they are not themselves judged true or false. When we reject a definite description as false we are in effect rejecting one or more previous sentences in which the description occurred as predicates prior to transfer to the subject. Thus, I might reject 'The old man living next door' in the sentence 'The old man living next door is tired' as false of its intended referent whom I now recognize as being young. If so, I would in effect be rejecting as false the earlier 'The man living next door is old' whose acceptance led to the transfer of the attribute expressed by 'old'.

The asymmetry between subjects and predicates with respect to falsity is similar to the asymmetry that Geach has noted holds for negation.[17] We can externally negate a sentence of the form 'S is P' with the sentence 'Not-(S is P)' or 'It is not the case that S is P'. This has the same logical meaning as the sentence 'S is not-P', with the negation applied directly to the predicate. There is no corresponding equivalence for the subject negation 'Not-S is P'. In certain special circumstances we do use sentences such as 'It is not John who is tired' with a negated subject. This occurs when there is a limited number of possible referents, and context functions to delimit the intended referent to give us the effect of 'It is not John who is tired, but instead . . .'. But for extended reference without such a context it is obvious that knowing what the intended referent is not will in itself be insufficient to enable an audience to identify what it is from among an indefinite number of possible referents. And even where there is a use for 'Not-S is P', its logical meaning would seem to be the same as the predicate negation from 'S is not-P'.[18]

In these discussions we have been employing the term 'object' (more properly, 'material object') as the correlate of a sentence's subject term. In Russell's program of analysis (cf. 1.1) objects are said to exist as the dyadic correlates of the 'real' logical subjects of sentences, as contrasted with the 'apparent' grammatical subjects. The goal of analysis is then to find a logical paraphrase of a given sentence in order to determine which objects its use commits us to claim exist. This program assumes, as we have seen, a time-invariant denotation relation which holds only for subjects within inferential contexts. For isolated sentences what determines existence? The answer seems to be that an object can be said to exist if the subject purporting to refer to it can enable an interpreter to identify what the speaker intends to refer to. The old man next door is an existing object if the term 'the old man next door' enables another to identify the intended referent, even if there is no individual which the description is true of. Moreover, if a given description happens in fact to be true of some one individual, this individual cannot be said to exist if it is impossible for identification of intended referent to at least be possible to take place.

This makes it possible to explain further the claim of 4.3 that neither natural signs nor signals can be said to stand for objects. The significance of both signs for their interpreters we have seen to be a type of event or feature which is recognized as occurring or not occurring at a referent occasion indicated by a particular sign token. But since they lack distinguishable subject terms, they cannot be said to be interpreted as referring to objects. Hence, for their interpreters objects do not exist. This seems paradoxical only because of the structure of the language we use in describing the interpretation of these more primitive signs.

These considerations also enable us, I think, to understand Wittgenstein's cryptic remarks about the status of sensations. A sentence such as 'I have a pain' seems to have the form of a relational sentence, with 'I' and 'a pain' referring to terms of the relation. But Wittgenstein seems to argue that the noun 'pain' is not a subject term with a referring role. Because we lack identity criteria and are hence incapable of identifying one pain as the same as another, the word 'pain' cannot be used to refer. If 'pain' is not a subject term, then there can be no object with which it is correlated. And similarly for every other noun that seems to refer to a sensation. A sensation, Wittgenstein says in the *Investigations*, 'is not a something, but it is also not a nothing.'[19] Sensations occur, Wittgenstein seems to be saying, but they are not objects referred to by subjects, since sensation nouns do not perform this function. The point is simply a logical one about the subject–predicate structure of avowals used to report sensations.

5.3 Meaning, truth and illocutionary force

We must distinguish between an interpreter's ability to understand a sentence used in speech or writing, its having meaning or significance for him, and his ability to specify its meaning. To understand a descriptive sentence such as 'John is gregarious' as used on a given occasion is to be able to identify the intended referent of its subject 'John' and judge whether the predicate 'is gregarious' is true or false of this referent. For an imperative such as 'Flagellate the prisoner' understanding occurs when the intended referent of 'the prisoner' can be identified and the interpreter knows what action must be performed to obey the imperative. To specify the meaning of these sentences or the words within them, on the other hand, is to provide a synonymous expression. Thus, the meaning of 'John is gregarious' can be said to be 'John is sociable' and 'flagellate' can be said to mean 'whip'. For certain adjectives like 'yellow' or 'bitter' no specification of meaning is possible. A person learns to understand them, but it makes no sense to ask for 'the meaning' of these words. The only answer would be to produce a synonym, and for them none can be given. In contrast, any noun will have criteria for identification associated with it which it is at least possible to specify. Obviously, it is only linguistic signs which have 'meaning' in the sense in which meaning can be specified. A natsign such as lightning has significance or meaning for an interpreter if he is capable of recognizing a significate occurrence or non-occurrence at the referent occasion. But it does not have 'meaning' in the sense that the word 'flagellate' does. And similarly for signals. These also have no 'meaning,' since to have meaning requires a linguistic framework in which it can be specified. A person can understand a linguistic expression, that is, be able to use it in the appropriate circumstances and judge it true or false or (if an imperative) obey or disobey it, without necessarily being able to specify its meaning. The latter ability requires a grasp of the stock of synonymous expressions available in a given language which the person may not have.

Corresponding to this ambiguity of 'meaning' there is also an ambiguity for the term 'interpretation'. We have been using the term with reference both to an agent's discrimination of a sign and recognition of a significate occurrence or non-occurrence and to the decision to perform or forbear from performing an action signified by the sign. But it can also be used to refer to the activity of specifying the meaning of a linguistic expression by replacing it by one more readily understood. Thus, I may 'interpret' someone's A's remarks to another B by either rephrasing them in different words within the same language or, if B fails to understand the language A is using, translate them into a language B does understand. There is also a third type of interpretation in which we specify more precisely what is expressed in an indefinite way, as we might interpret someone's remark 'I am going abroad soon' to mean 'I am going to Europe within the next month'. Here we select 'Europe' and 'within the next month' from a range of possible interpretations of the indefinite expressions 'abroad' and 'soon'. Obviously, these second and third senses of 'interpretation' are language-relative in a way the first and more general sense is not. In the second and third senses we can interpret what a person says in total disregard of its truth or a decision to perform an action. In the first sense, to interpret is simply to make either judgments of truth or practical decisions.

One type of specification of meaning (or interpretation) is logical paraphrase of the kind provided by Russell's program of logical analysis. To say that 'The present king of France is bald' means 'There is exactly one king of France and he is bald' is to specify the meaning of the singular sentence in terms of a general sentence which can be represented by the symbolism of modern logic. The latter also can be regarded as stating the conditions under which the former is true. Hence the formula of the analytic program: to know the meaning of a sentence is to know its truth conditions.[20] To represent the logical form of a sentence is thought to state its truth conditions and justify the inference to the totality of consequences derivable from the sentence as a means of testing its truth or falsity. We have already criticized this view, in Section 1.1, noting that a single logical representation can only be adequate for justifying a certain sub-set of the indefinite number of consequences that can be inferred.

Another goal of the program of logical analysis not so far discussed is that of employing a paraphrase and logical representation to reveal how the meaning of a sentence is a function of the meaning of its constituent words plus their mode of combination. Words such as nouns, adjectives, and verbs are regarded as logically simple meaningful elements which have independent meaning. The logical connectives 'not', 'and', 'or', 'implies', etc. then become operators which when applied to simple atomic sentences formed from these words generate complex wholes whose relation to their parts are exhibited. The search for a method of forming complexes from simples can be seen as a project starting with Locke's analysis of complex ideas into simple ideas and continuing with phenomenalism's 'construction' of objects from immediate sensations or sense data. For the program of logical analysis complex sentences are the wholes, words the simple parts, and logical operations plus sentence-forming rules their mode of combination. In some reductionist versions of the program the elementary simples were words standing for data of immediate experience, e.g. 'red', 'bitter', 'round', etc.

This program has never been successfully carried out, and it is not difficult to see why. In fact, words do not have meaning in isolation from the discourse and sentence contexts in which they occur. As we saw in 4.4, even a word such as 'red' has a meaning dependent on a partitioning of the semantic field in which it is positioned, a partitioning which can vary with the purposes with which the word is used. Further, it is often noted that relative adjectives such as 'big' and 'small' have meanings which vary with the nouns they modify: 'big' in 'big mouse' has a different meaning from its occurence in 'big elephant'. Similar shifts in meaning can depend on entire sentence contexts: 'running' in the sentence 'My nose is running' has a different meaning from its occurrence in 'The horse is running'. Attempts have been made to distinguish idioms without semantic structure from sentences with a meaning structured from combinations of meaningful words. But as David Cooper points out, there are many examples of sentences which are not idioms and yet are not structured combinations of the kind seemed by this program of analysis.[21] Within the framework of language the meanings of words are altered by their combinations and the uses made of the sentences in which they occur.

If elements out of which sentences are formed are not the simples of logical analysis, where can they be found? The answer advocated by the program of semiotic outlined in this work should be clear. The simple–complex distinction for semiotic is not at the level of language and sentences as linguistic signs. Instead, the distinction can be drawn by means of the vertical relations between sentences and signs at the more primitive levels of signals and natsigns. We understand how sentences are used and interpreted, not by isolating their constituent words and rules of combination, but by abstracting from them features unique to the interpretation of linguistic signs in order to derive the basic features of successively more primitive varieties of signs.

The analysis of a sentence's meaning in terms of truth conditions can be interpreted, as we have done above, as providing another sentence synonymous with the original. But it can also be given a realist interpretation in which the sentence is an iconic representation of that which is described in stating truth conditions. The meaning of any iconic sign is the respect by which it is similar to what it signifies, as the meaning of a drawing of a man is the respect in which it is similar to that man. The meaning of a sentence is now regarded as the respect by which it is similar or 'corresponds' to what is called the 'fact' or 'state of affairs' it signifies. To specify the meaning of a sentence is to describe this fact by stating the conditions under which the sentence is true by means of Tarski's formula:

A sentence 'S' is true if and only if S

in which 'S' mentions a sentence and S describes the state of affairs to which it corresponds.[22] The respect by which a sentence such as 'John is tall' represents the fact that John is tall is obviously different from that with which a drawing represents a man. Nevertheless, the so-called 'correspondence theory' of truth insists on their being such a representational relation, perhaps one of some kind of general structural similarity, and holds that truth can be ascribed when the relation is present.

In Section 4.2 we criticized what is called the 'redundancy' or 'performative' theory of truth which claims that to say of an utterance of a sentence that it is true is simply to accept or assert that sentence. There we argued that acceptance is analogous to recognition of a significate occurrence, and this latter psychological act can occur without there being an ascription of truth, as happens for non-conventional signals and natsigns. But this criticism should not be taken as an endorsement of the rival correspondence theory. The terms 'fact' and 'state of affairs' are simply technical philosophic terms introduced to provide a correlate to the term 'sentence', and it seems obvious that they stand for nothing that independently exists. Someone says 'This table is brown', and I agree, having identified the intended referent and judged that what I perceive is of the type signified by the predicate 'is brown'. But independent of me there are not two entities, one the table as an object, the other the quality of brownness inhering in it, nor is there a state of affairs of the table being brown. There is one entity, the table, the referent of the sentence's subject as used on that occasion and identified by the hearer if communication is successful. The subject–predicate distinction is a functional one, evolving, as we have seen, as a means of extending the referent occasion. It has absolutely no ontological import, contrary to the claims of the correspondence theory. There is no temptation to introduce states of affairs in describing the interpretation of natsigns and signals. There should be none when the interpretation is directed towards utterances of sentences, despite the added complexity of structure introduced at this level.

So far we have restricted discussion to the meaning expressed by the subject–predicate structure of a sentence. We saw in 4.3 how features of signals such as pitch, intensity, and frequency of repetition can be used by communicators to convey the illocutionary force with which they are intended. At the level of language illocutionary force can also be conveyed by distinguishable parts of sentences. The easiest to identify are the performative prefixes first noted by Austin, prefixes such as 'I warn you that . . .', 'I state that . . .', 'I question whether . . .', etc. which express the force of the subject–predicate radical that follows, that is, indicate whether it is being used as a warning, statement, question, etc. Thus, 'I warn you that John is coming' and 'I state that John is coming' contain prefixes which indicate that the content expressed by the radical 'John is coming' is to be understood as a warning and a statement. For an imperative such as 'Close the door' illocutionary force is also indicated by performative prefixes. Thus, we form 'I request you to close the door' and 'I order you to close the door' as a means of indicating that closing the door is being requested and ordered. As for signals, intonation and stress are available as 'natural' indicators of illocutionary force. The addition of verbal expressions at the level of sentences has the advantage of enabling indefinitely greater explicitness and precision in conveying how a given content is to be understood.

Characteristic of performative prefixes, as Austin notes, is that one who uses them is performing the speech acts of warning, stating, questioning, requesting, ordering, etc. that they express.[23] But illocutionary force can also be conveyed by other linguistic expressions, including some psychological prefixes and verbs such as 'seems' and 'appears'. To say 'I think that John is coming' and 'I believe that John is coming' is to indicate some qualifications or hesitancy in asserting that John is coming. In contrast, to say 'I know that John is coming' is to convey that this content is to be taken as guaranteed. Similarly, to say 'This table appears (seems, looks) brown' is to qualify what would be asserted by saying 'This table is brown' in a confident tone of voice.

Sentences such as 'I warn you that John is coming' have meanings to which performative prefixes or other verbal devices contribute. For such sentences we can distinguish the meaning in the sense of literal meaning expressed by the subject–predicate radical from the meaning expressed by the prefix. Like the sentence-predicate radical the illocutionary force indicator is rule-governed and conventional. But it seems related to the force it expresses in a different way. Recall from 4.2 that for a conventional sign the intentions of the communicator do not alter the meaning which the sign expresses. If someone says 'Blue' intending to mean by the word what is conventionally meant by 'Red', the meaning of what he says is not what he intends it to mean, even if this intention were successfully recognized by his audience. The meaning of such an utterance is a function of the rule-governed type of which it is a token, not the intentions with which the particular utterance is produced. In contrast, suppose that this person were to say 'I order you to close the door' intending by the utterance not an order but a request. Then if his audience were to recognize this intention, it would seem that the utterance has the force of a request rather than an order and that the illocutionary speech act of requesting has been successfully performed. Illocutionary force is thus dependent on the speaker's intentions and their recognition in a way that the literal meaning of a radical is not.

In this respect, then, illocutionary force is like reference, varying with the intentions of the speaker at the occasion of utterance. It must be emphasized that when intended force varies from what is normally understood by a verbal illocutionary force indicator the meanings of these indicators do not themselves change. Because a person says 'I order you to . . .' but intends a request, it does not follow that 'order' is now synonymous with 'request'. The word instead retains its conventional meaning. But this simply demonstrates that illocutionary force is not to be identified with the conventional meaning of these verbal indicators. The latter is instead only a means of making the former understood. Normally, a person in using a performative verb or other verbal illocutionary indicator will intend its conventional meaning. This is usually the most effective way of insuring that his intentions will in fact be recognized. Certainly in long-distance communication where intonation, stress, and context may not be available as communicative devices, this coincidence will be almost always indispensable for success. But the coincidence is not essential, and where there is divergence illocutionary force seems determined by recognized intention.

The expression of illocutionary force is a feature of comsigns having no analogue at the level of natsigns. Another special feature was also noted in 4.3, the presence of aspects of comsigns by which both the source and intended target of the sign are communicated. At the level of sentences this feature introduces problems that warrant special discussion, and to them we now turn.

5.4 Addresses

The most obvious examples of addresses within sentences are names indicating the addressee of a given indicative or imperative. Thus, we say 'John, the door is closed' as a way of indicating that it is John for whom the information about the door is intended or 'John, close the door' as indicating that it is to John that the command is addressed. Clearly the function of the name 'John' in both sentences is very different from the subject term 'the door'. The latter is used to refer to the object being described or to be acted on, while the name does not refer to what is to be identified. Instead, it has the very different function of alerting the person for whom the information or command is intended.[24] In face-to-face conversations we rarely find addresses indicating who the source of a given message is; normally, sound direction and the speaker's movements suffice. But in telephone conversations these are usually necessary, and we find such locutions as 'John, this is Peter', with 'John' as before indicating the addressee and now 'Peter' indicating the addressor, the source of the message to follow.

It is a common error to confuse the address of an imperative with one of its subjects. In R.M. Hare's analysis of imperatives, for example, the imperative '(You) close the door' with the implicit second person pronoun is said to correspond to and have the same subject–predicate structure as the indicative 'You close the door' in which 'you' and the 'the door' are subjects.[25] But clearly the functions of 'the door' and the implicit 'you' in the imperative are different. The definite description 'the door' is used to orient or direct the action of closing being commanded, to enable the hearer to identify the independent object upon which the action is to be performed. No function even remotely analogous to this is performed by the implicit 'you' or by a name such as 'John' if explicitly prefixed. Certainly no confusion of function is made for indicatives, where we can clearly distinguish the functions of 'John' as address and 'the door' as subject in 'John, the door is closed'. None then should be made where the sentence is in the imperative mood.

The function of addresses is not restricted simply to indicating source and target. Often there will be features of an utterance that also serve to indicate the relative social status of speaker and hearer. As we noted in 4.3, voice pitch serves to distinguish female from male human speakers, much as features of signals in animal communication function as signatures of sex and species. Such features as a deferential or haughty tone of voice can also indicate relationships of class inferiority or superiority. Titles such as 'Professor' and 'Dr' and forms of address such as 'Mr', 'Mrs', and 'Ms' are verbal devices for indicating the status of the addressee. In Japanese honorifics and verb forms have the function of indicating adult–child and other superior–inferior relationships.

But it is not only features of utterances and linguistic forms that performs this addressing role. At least as early as Kant there has been recognition of the role of non-linguistic devices such as clothing and insignias as addresses characterizing those that wear or display them.[26] Writers in the European semiological tradition (cf. 2.4) have extended this list to include perfumes, cooking, and an indefinite number of other culturally significant non-linguistic signs of status. Thus, men and women indicate sexual availability by gait, gestures, clothing, perfumes, and the presence or absence of wedding rings. Social status is indicated by size and decor of homes, food and beverages served, table settings, clothing, manners, etc. All of these non-verbal devices clearly have a very different role from that of ascribing some attribute to some independent object to be identified or of prescribing an action. Not to be confused with the subject–predicate radicals used to refer to ascribe and prescribe, they nevertheless perform an important communicative function. It is precisely because, unlike subject terms, they are not used to extend the referent occasion and allow the storage of increasingly precise information that they can perform this function by non-linguistic means.[27]

The occurrence of the first person pronoun 'I' as the grammatical subject of sentences has been the source of metaphysical beliefs about the soul or mind as an entity to which experiences are ascribed, beliefs that have caused much philosophical mischief. This can be avoided by a proper understanding of the pronoun's function. Used in conjunction with an address the first person pronoun is invariably used as a substitute for a speaker address. The expression 'This is Peter. I am standing at Main and Poplar' as used in a phone conversation contains the pronoun 'I' standing in place of the address 'Peter'. It is what Geach calls a 'pronoun of laziness' that could be replaced by the proper name. 'You', in contrast, occurs in combination with an address indicating the addressee, as in the indicative 'Tom, you are sitting by a fire' or the imperative 'Tom, you close the door'.

But in addition to having this addressing function as stand-ins for names the pronouns seem also to have additional roles. The 'I' in 'I am standing' if said by Peter expresses for the hearer what could be expressed by 'Peter is standing', and is used by the hearer to identify the person to whom the predicate is to be ascribed. Similarly, the 'you' in 'You are sitting by a fire' if addressed to John is used by the speaker to refer to John as the individual who is sitting. The pronouns thus have at least some of the characteristics associated with the subjects of a sentence. But addresses we have just maintained have a function very different from that of subjects. How can these pronouns function both as stand-ins for addresses and as subjects of the sentences in which they occur?

To answer this requires our reviewing two features of subject terms discussed in 5.1. They are first of all used by the speaker to refer to the object or objects to which the predicate is intended to be ascribed. Second, they are used by the audience to identify an object or objects to which to ascribe the predicate. Standard subject terms combine both uses, with successful communication realized only when the speaker's intended referent is the object actually identified by the audience. But there is no logical reason why a given expression with one of these features must also have the other. By a *quasi-subject* we shall mean an expression which has only one of the two features, either a speaker-referring use or an audience-identifying use, but not both. Such expressions do exist, and indeed are represented by first and second person pronouns.

That the first person 'I' is not used by the speaker to refer seems obvious from its occurrences within performatives. As Austin noted, to say 'I promise that the money will be returned' is not to make an assertion, nor for the speaker to predicate a kind of promise of himself as referred to by 'I'. The subject of the performative as used by the speaker is the expression 'the money', not the first person pronoun, which merely serves along with context to indicate the source of the promise. Warnock contends that explicit performatives such as 'I promise that *p*' express true or false propositions describing the action expressed by the performative verb. But this cannot be so. For suppose the performative does express a proposition *p*, say the proposition that the speaker is promising that *p*. Then it could in turn have its illocutionary force indicated by a performative prefix to form a sentence such as 'I state that I promise that *p*'. This expression could in turn be regarded as expressing a proposition *q* occurring in another performative such as 'I warn you that *q*', and so on for an infinite number of performatives embedded in wider performatives. Such embedding does not in fact occur in natural languages. What Warnock may have in mind is the fact that corresponding to the performative 'I promise that *p*' there is the third person indicative 'He promises that *p*' which is true or false depending on whether or not the conditions for successful performance of the speech act are fulfilled. While the 'I' in the performative is not used by the speaker to refer, it is used by the hearer to identify who is making the promise prior to asserting the corresponding third person indicative. The pronoun is thus a quasi-subject.

But it is not only in performatives that it plays this role. Indeed, in virtually all occurrences 'I' seems to have the unique feature of functioning for hearer identification but not speaker reference. We have seen how in the phone conversation 'This is Peter. I am standing at Main and Poplar' the speaker is not using the pronoun to refer to himself, but in place of his name as the address. It is used by the hearer, however, as a quasi-subject identifying who it is that is standing at the corner. For psychological predicates this hybrid use of 'I' also occurs. In 'I am tired' used in face-to-face communication the pronoun indicates the speaker as the source of the utterance directly to the hearer. The speaker is not using the pronoun to refer to some mysterious subject of experiences, but instead as an address. The hearer, in contrast, uses the pronoun and the speech context to identify that to which the psychological predicate is to be ascribed.

In arguing for the non-referring use of 'I' Anscombe notes two features of the pronoun that differ markedly from singular subjects. Standard subjects, e.g. names, definite descriptions, and noun phrases with demonstratives, can be used by the speaker without his or her knowing to which object it applies. They can also be used in situations where the object the speaker intends to refer to does not exist. Anscombe draws the conclusion, and quite correctly, that since 'I' shares neither of these features it is not a referring expression.[28] But for the audience these features are present in the interpretation of the pronoun. I may hear someone say 'I am tired' and, not knowing the source of the utterance, fail to correctly identify the individual to which the predicate is being ascribed. Further, the sound I hear may be produced by an artificial device and there may not exist any such individual. For the audience, at least, the pronoun does indeed have the features essential for a subject term.

Wittgenstein's dual use theory draws a sharp contrast between the use of 'I' in sentences with physical and psychological predicates.[29] In a sentence such as 'I am standing' it is a referring expression replaceable by 'my body'. But in 'I am tired' its use, Wittgenstein maintained, is very different. Here 'I' occurs only as a grammatical subject with no logical function to fulfill, much like the 'it' of 'It is raining'. In this way he thought he could avoid the need to postulate a subject of experiences as the referent of the pronoun.

This view is, however, implausible. Certainly there are occasions where 'I' and 'my body' are interchangeable, as 'I (my body) am (is) covered with blisters', but these are atypical. Certainly 'My body is standing' sounds very unnatural, and seems to be not equivalent to the first person version. The reason for this is that the latter is not being used by the speaker to refer to anything, but is used instead to indicate the speaker as the source of the message. For the avowal 'I am tired' Wittgenstein seems equally mistaken. If the pronoun were simply a grammatical filler, then the sentence would be equivalent to 'Tired'. But the adjective used by itself would make it impossible for the hearer to identify what the psychological state expressed by the verb is to be ascribed to, precisely the role fulfilled by 'I' as a quasi-subject. There are thus no grounds for distinguishing two uses of 'I' that differ with the two types of predicates. For neither type is the pronoun used to refer, and for both types it functions to enable hearer identification.

Much of the plausibility of Strawson's theory of persons as a unique type of 'basic particular' to which both physical and psychological predicates are ascribed stems from the apparent equivalence between first and third person sentences. 'I am tired' said *by* me and 'He is tired' said by another *of* me both seem to express the same proposition with the same truth conditions. This in turn seems to require both of their pronoun subjects to have the same reference. The situation is the same where we have physical predicates, as in 'I am standing' and 'He is standing' said of me as speaker. If there is propositional equivalence in both cases, it seems reasonable to postulate a common referent, and for Strawson the person fills this role.[30] I hope the foregoing is sufficient to disclose the fallacy committed here. The performative 'I promise that *p*' cannot be equivalent to 'He promises that *p*' simply because the use by the speaker of 'I' is not a referring use. For the hearer, on the other hand, the equivalence does hold. This contrast extends generally to all occurrences of the pronoun.

Almost totally ignored by writers has been the functioning of the second person 'you' as complementing the first person pronoun. Clearly, 'you' as occurring in sentences such as 'You are standing' and 'You are tired' is used by the speaker both to refer to an individual and as an address. It is the person addressed of whom the predicates are being ascribed. But for the hearer only the addressing function is relevant, there being no object to identify prior to ascribing the predicates. The hearer is not identifying his own body to ascribe the physical predicate, since 'My body is standing' again does not seem equivalent in meaning, nor is it possible, as we have known since Hume, to identify a subject for the psychological predicate. Like 'I', 'you' is a quasi-subject with only one of the two functions performed by a standard subject. This time, however, it is the identifying rather than the referring function that is absent. Here the speaker may fail to know to whom he is referring if the hearer is hidden from view and there may even be no referent, only some mechanical noise-producing device which the speaker is addressing. But for the hearer no such break-downs can possibly occur, and the pronoun thus has an addressing function.

Since 'I' and 'you' are not used to refer under the special circumstances just described, their use does not presuppose the existence of a special type of object ontologically distinct from material bodies. What are identified by the hearer in hearing 'I' and referred to by the speaker in using 'you' are other persons as material bodies encountered in communicative situations. We thus have the advantage of ontological simplicity, without the implausibility of requiring differing uses of the pronouns with psychological and physical predicates.

5.5 Discourse

So far we have restricted attention to sentences as individual units of communication. We turn now to special features introduced when sentences are combined to form a discourse. A discourse can be verbal, e.g. a speech, sermon, debate, conversation, etc., or written, a text such as a letter, directive, technical paper, or book. For the purposes of our very summary account the differences between these forms are inessential.

In some cases the parts of a discourse serve to illustrate and make more explicit some of the features discussed in the preceding sections. For example, parts of a written letter or memo function as its address. The salutation and heading of a letter and the 'memo to' section of a memo indicate the intended reader and often his or her social status and location. The close of a letter and the 'from' section of a memo with their dates and return address indicate the name, status, and location of the writer, as well as the date at which the message is sent.[31] Often within a discourse a separate sentence will serve to convey the intended illocutionary force of the entire discourse, as when we find sentences such as 'This is a warning' or 'This is a request' inserted within a text. In abbreviated form this occurs in 'No Trespassing' signs saying 'Warning. Trespassers will be prosecuted'.

Also illustrated in a more explicit way is the phenomenon of information transfer from predicates to subjects discussed in Section 5.1. Consider as an example a simple narrative discourse consisting of the following three sentences: 'Peter is tall. He has blond hair. Peter is also fat'. For one who believes in the veracity of the speaker (or writer) and accepts the sentences as true, the significance of 'Peter' will have changed from its occurrence in the first sentence to its occurrence in the last. With no prior information about the individual the name 'Peter' signifies through the noun category to which it belongs only a male human. After interpreting the discourse the information conveyed by the predicates 'has blond hair' and 'fat' becomes transferred to the name and alters its significance. It now could be replaced by the definite description 'the man who has blond hair and is fat' expressing the attributes to be used in identifying a given individual as Peter. In Section 5.1 this transference was described as taking place for sentences used at discontinuous occasions. Here the transference occurs for sentences arranged sequentially within a single discourse.

Such transference can also occur for sentences within a prescriptive discourse as a sequence of related commands or instructions, e.g. a cooking recipe, do-it-yourself carpentry instructions, repair procedures, etc. A recipe might contain instructions such as 'Add salt to the batter. Stir it thoroughly. Then bake the batter at 450 degrees Fahrenheit'. As for the narrative example just given, the significance of the subject 'the batter' is changed from its occurrence in the first sentence to its occurrence in the last. Initially it is synonymous with something such as 'the paste-like mixture of flour and water'; in its last occurrence it becomes 'the paste-like mixture of flour and water to which salt has been added and has been stirred thoroughly'. It is this complex description which is used to identify the object after the initial adding and stirring instructions have been carried out. In this way the subjects of imperatives within prescriptive discourse express changing criteria for identifying objects upon which actions are to be sequentially performed. The predicates expressing earlier actions in the sequence become incorporated into successively more complex descriptions by which objects are identified at later stages.

While addresses, illocutionary force, and information transfer may be illustrated in amplified form by examples of discourse, other features can be significantly altered. An example of this we already noted in Section 1.1 in the outline of the program of logical analysis. We saw there that within inferential contexts we can assume constancy of truth value for all sentences expressing the same proposition, in contrast to isolated occasion sentences such as 'John is sitting' whose truth or falsity will vary when used at different times and places. Also assumed for inferences is constancy of reference for subjects, while for sentences outside such contexts the reference of subject terms can vary with both the occasion of use and intentions of their users.

Still another assumption (not discussed in 1.1) is introduced when we evaluate inferences as valid or invalid. For such evaluation it is possible to assume that all propositions expressed by sentences within inferential contexts are either true or false, that is, assume what is called the 'principle of bivalence.' This assumption is made possible by the fact that in evaluating an inference we are only determining whether it is *possible* for its premisses to be true and its conclusion false. If this is possible, the inference is invalid; if not, it is valid. Such evaluation does not require us to assert either premisses or conclusion as *actually* true or false. There may be sentences which because of insufficient evidence we are unable to assert or accept as true or false, e.g. the sentence 'On no other planet in our solar system besides Earth are there living organisms'. But we are able to evaluate inferences in which such a sentence occurs as valid or invalid. For example, the inference,

On no other planet in our solar system besides Earth are there living organisms

Mars is a planet in our solar system
_____
On Mars there are no living organisms

would certainly be evaluated as valid, for if the first premiss were true along with the second, the conclusion would follow. The fact that we can neither assert nor deny its first premiss as an independent sentence does not require us to abandon the principle of bivalence when we assign possible truth values in evaluating the inference in which it occurs. Some philosophers have concluded from the applicability of the bivalence principle that for every given sentence there is a determinate state of affairs to which it either corresponds or fails to correspond. If it corresponds, it is true; otherwise, it is false. On these grounds they distinguish the truth of a sentence from its assertion on a given occasion. But this is to mistakenly take a logical principle which holds only for the special circumstances of inference evaluation as a principle that applies to all descriptive sentences. The correspondence theory of truth which we criticized in 5.3 thus represents the failure to recognize the uniqueness of a feature which holds only of sentences in inferential contexts.[32]

Scientific theories present another discourse context which introduces a second feature not generally holding of sentences outside it. Descriptive sentences have traditionally been classified into empirical *synthetic* sentences, sentences accepted as true or denied as false relative to empirical evidence, and *analytic* sentences, those whose assertion or denial is based only on the meanings of certain key constituent words. Thus, 'It is raining' is a synthetic sentence; 'It is raining or not raining', on the other hand, is analytic, since we assert its truth on the basis of the meaning of the words 'or' and 'not'. But as has been known since the writings of Poincaré at the beginning of this century and emphasized more recently by Quine,[33] within the context of scientific theories it is possible to find general sentences which cannot be classified as either analytic or synthetic. The three basic laws of Newton's theory of gravitation are:

For all material bodies
  (1) $a = 0$, if no external force is exerted (the law of inertia)
  (2) $F = m \times a$ (the force–mass–acceleration law)
  (3) $F = G \times Mm/r^2$ (the inverse square law).

Neither of the first two of these sentences can be empirically tested in isolation. Yet (1) does not seem to be merely a definition of the term 'acceleration', nor is (2) a definition of 'force' in terms of 'mass' and 'acceleration'. Neither sentence is therefore synthetic or analytic. Newton's theory as the *conjunction* of the three sentences, however, can be empirically tested, and we can at least say of this theory that it is synthetic. Thus, the analytic–synthetic classification can be applied to a theory, but not to individual sentences within it.

From this some have concluded that the analytic–synthetic distinction cannot be applied to *any* single sentence, whether or not it occurs within a theoretical context. This is plainly false. 'It is raining' is surely synthetic; on the basis of direct observation it can be asserted. On the other hand, the sentence 'If it is raining and cloudy then it is raining' of the form (A & B) ⊃ A is just as plainly analytic. Given the meanings of 'and' and 'if . . . then' it could not possibly be denied. To deny that the analytic–synthetic distinction applies to these sentences is to confuse the status of sentences within theoretical contexts with those outside such a context.[34]

Still another feature unique to discourse contexts is to be found in fictional narrations. Here information transference from predicates to subjects occurs of the kind just discussed above for non-fictional narrative discourse. Thus, a novelist may write 'The old man walked with a limp. He wore a blue suit with a red necktie. He smiled frequently'. If then the novelist continues 'The old man knocked at the door', this last occurrence of 'the old man' is synonymous with the definite description 'the old man who walked with a limp, wore a blue suit and red necktie, and smiled frequently' in which occurs the predicates of the sentences that preceded. For the novelist to 'develop a character' is for the meaning of a name or definite description to change from earlier occurrences in the discourse to later. A term within a fictional narration can be termed a *structural subject term* when it occupies the position of a sentence's subject. Such a subject exploits the mechanisms of information transference which operate wherever there are repeated occurrences of a subject followed by a variety of predicates. It is not, however, a *functional subject*, one which is used to refer to some object to be identified. There is, of course, no spatial or temporal occasion at which such identification could or could not have taken place, and without this possibility there is no reference.

We must reject, then, any theory which attempts to assign referents to fictional subjects. This obviously applies to Meinong's theory of 'subsistents' as referents of a term such as 'Pegasus' in 'Pegasus is white', in contrast to 'existents' as referents of ordinary proper names such as 'Aristotle' and 'John F. Kennedy'. It also applies to Russell's theory outlined in Section 1.1 in which 'Pegasus' is first replaced by a definite description, e.g. 'the winged horse captured by Bellerophon' to form the sentence 'The winged horse captured by Bellerophon is white'. As outlined in 1.1, a new subject 'material thing', the 'true' logical subject, is then introduced, and the sentence is paraphrased by an existential sentence in which 'is a winged horse captured by Bellerophon' and 'is white' are predicates. Still more recent theories postulate a possible world in which exists an individual named 'Pegasus' and satisfying the unique attributes expressed by the associated definite description. The task set for all such theories is to specify the referent of the fictional sentence 'Pegasus is white'. But this is to assume that sentences within discourse contexts function in all respects as do sentences isolated from them, and we have seen this not to be the case. Just because subjects of isolated descriptive sentences are used to refer, it does not at all follow that subjects of sentences within fictional discourse must also have this function.

Some may object to this attempt to distinguish features of discourse-relative sentences from isolated sentences by arguing that *all* sentences occur in the context of some discourse or other. Even a sentence such as 'It is raining' normally occurs in the context of a conversation, and is an answer to at least an implied question ('What is the weather like?'). An 'isolated sentence' is therefore a fiction, and cannot sustain a contrast to a sentence within a discourse context.

The contention being made is, of course, correct, but does not constitute an objection to the contrasts we have been drawing. Developed forms of discourse – whether inferences, scientific theories, novels, directives, or laws, etc. – are employed for specific social purposes, and their special features derive from these purposes. The sentences that occur in everyday conversation, in contrast, are used for a variety of purposes, and their principal features enable this flexibility. By an 'isolated sentence' has been meant a sentence with this potential flexibility of use. The error committed by the theories so far discussed has been either that of projecting features of a specialized use of language on to sentences with a potential for a variety of uses or of ascribing to a specialized use (as in fiction) what holds of sentences for which flexibility is essential.

There are thus dangers in restricting analysis – as has been the practice of much recent philosophy – to the relatively complex language forms to be found in developed areas of discourse, dangers which often outweigh the advantages of the explicitness and amplification these complex forms provide. We have seen in this chapter how generalizing from features of discourse-relative sentences can lead to distorted views of reference, meaning, and truth. The remedy is to adopt the strategy followed in the last three chapters and focus attention on features of language shared in common between relatively simple sentences and more primitive types of signs.

POSTCRIPT

Our discussion of language forms has been cursory and partial. There has only been brief mention of general sentences and only an indefinite sketch of a few forms of discourse. I have ignored the special features of first person avowals, whether expressive of feelings and emotions such as 'I feel tired' and 'I am sad' or reports of sensations such as 'I feel a pain'. As forms of language parasitic on ordinary descriptive language their use poses special problems. There has been no mention of the iconic symbolic forms characteristic of artistic expression, nor of the symbolic formulas employed in mathematics.

There is a good practical reason, I think, for excluding these more complex signs from the scope of semiotic as conceived of in this work. It is simply that the study of signs at these higher levels of complexity becomes indistinguishable from established branches of philosophy such as the philosophy of language, deductive and inductive logic, philosophy of science, philosophy of mathematics, philosophy of law, and aesthetics. There is nothing unique that semiotic has to offer regarding the structures and use and interpretation of these forms of discourse studied by other branches. Instead, its focus is properly on features of language revealed by contrasts and comparisons between simple forms of sentences and more primitive signs.

There is, however, what might be called a 'semiotic perspective' that can be brought to bear on the study of more complex lansigns. It consists of extending the focus on comparative features of the kind developed in this work for singular sentences and primitive signs to those holding between singular sentences and sentences embedded in the various frameworks of discourse. The previous section may provide some indication as to how this extension is to be made. How does the reference of terms such as 'quark' and 'neutrino' standing for theoretical entities postulated by a physical theory differ from that of singular terms such as

137

'this book' as occurring in 'This book is red'? How does information transference to such terms as a result of confirmation of a theory in which they occur compare with that discussed in the previous chapter for singular terms? How do the iconic representations of paintings or other forms of artistic expression compare to the gestures or sounds of primitive iconic comsigns? But though such questions may be generated by extending the study outlined in this work, answers to them we should expect to find in the branches of philosophy linked to the special forms of discourse.

Notes

1 Introduction

1 See Russell's *Introduction to Mathematical Philosophy*, London, Allen & Unwin, 1919, Ch. XVII. Russell's interests in logical analysis at this early stage were ontological. Specifically, by replacing a sentence's grammatical subject by its logical subject he sought to show the kinds of objects denoted by the sentence. For later developments of this same project see Gilbert Ryle, 'Systematically Misleading Expressions' in R. Rorty (ed.), *The Linguistic Turn*, Chicago, Chicago University Press, 1967 and W.V.O. Quine, 'On What There Is' in *A Logical Point of View*, New York, Harper & Row, 1953. Later Russell, in common with the early Wittgenstein and Carnap, used logical representation techniques as a devise for pursuing the epistemic goal of analyzing complex propositions into simple atomic propositions reporting the immediate data of experience. For this project see his 'The Philosophy of Logical Atomism' in *Logic and Knowledge*, New York, Capricorn, 1956.

2 See 'On Referring,' *Mind*, 59 (1950): 30-44. Strawson introduces the term 'reference' to stand for the triadic relation between a subject term and an object as used by a person on a given occasion in contrast to the logician's term 'denotation' as standing for a dyadic relation between subject and object in abstraction from such use.

3 More exactly, $\exists x(Kx \ \& \ \forall y(Ky \supset y = x) \ \& \ Bx)$ logically entails $\exists xKx$, $\exists x \forall y(Ky \supset y = x)$, and $\exists xBx$. Since $\exists xKx$ is false, it follows that $\exists x(Kx \ \& \ \forall y(Ky \supset y = x) \ \& \ Bx)$ must be false.

4 See Donald Davidson, 'The Logical Form of Action Sentences' in N. Rescher (ed.), *The Logic of Decision and Action*, Pittsburgh, University of Pittsburgh Press, 1967. The example used here is from Gilbert Harman's exposition of Davidson's theory in 'Logical Form' in Davidson and Harman (eds), *The Logic of Grammar*, Eicino, Dickenson, 1975. Davidson's, project is again briefly discussed below in Section 5.3.

5 Exactly such a distinction is argued for by Strawson in 'Grammar and Philosophy' in his *Logico-Linguistic Papers*, London, Methuen, 1971. Here the contrast is made between the 'essential grammar' of 'non-empirical linguistics,' i.e. philosophy, and the transformational grammar of a given language as constructed by the procedures of empirical linguistics.

6 In his *Philosophy of Language*, New York, Harper & Row, 1966, Ch. 3, and *The Underlying Reality of Language and Its Philosophic Import*, New York, Harper & Row, 1971, Chs 1-3, Jerrold Katz argues that there is no distinction, that the features of language sought by both the philosophical traditions of logical analysis and ordinary language descriptions are deep structures of language discovered by the empirical procedures of transformational grammar. For the equation of logical form with the linguists' deep structure see also Gilbert Harman, 'Deep Structure as Logical Form' and George Lakoff, 'Linguistics and Natural Logic,' both in Davidson and Harman (eds), *Semantics of Natural Language*, Dordrecht, D. Reidel, 1972.

7 For this criticism see Michael Dummett, 'Can Analytical Philosophy be Systematic and Ought it to Be?' in his *Truth and Other Enigmas*, London, Duckworth, 1978. The ordinary language philosophers, claims Dummett, espouse a 'doctrine of total particularism' in their descriptions of the various uses of sentences.

8 Cf. Max Black, *Models and Metaphors*, Ithaca, Cornell University Press, 1962, p. 241: 'By an *archetype* I mean a systematic repertoire of ideas by means of which a given thinker describes, by *analogical extension*, some domain to which those ideas do not immediately and literally apply.'

9 For a discussion of the link between sign complexity and evolution see T.P. Waldron, *Principles of Language and Mind*, London, Routledge & Kegan Paul, 1985.

10 See Zenon Pylyshyn, *Computation and Cognition*, Cambridge, Mass., MIT Press, 1984 and Steven Stich, *From Folk Psychology to Cognitive Science*, Cambridge, Mass., MIT Press, 1983. I present here a version of what Stich calls the 'sentential theory' of psychological attitudes. According to this theory, for one to have an intentional attitude (a belief or desire) 'is to have a sentence token suitably instantiated or encoded in one's brain' (p. 29).

11 Paul Churchland, *Scientific Realism and the Plasticity of Mind*, Cambridge, Cambridge University Press, 1979, pp. 128ff. Extending investigations in the way Churchland proposes is to adopt the program of what Jerry Fodor calls 'naturalistic psychology' and accept the challenge (which Fodor claims cannot in practice be met in the foreseeable future) of correlating internal signs with environmental stimuli and behavioral effects. See Fodor's 'Methodological Solipsism Considered as a Research Strategy in Cognitive Psychology,' *The Behavioral and Brain Sciences*, 3 (1980): 63-73.

2 History of semiotic

1 For good general summaries of this early history see Umberto Eco, *Semiotics and the Philosophy of Language*, Bloomington, Indiana University Press, 1984, Sections 1.6 and 1.7 and Thomas Sebeok,

'Semiotics: A Survey of the State of the Art' in his *Contributions to the Doctrine of Signs*, Bloomington, Indiana University Press, 1976. More specialized studies can be found in A. Eschbach and J. Trabant (eds), *History of Semiotic*, Amsterdam, Verlag, 1983. Sebeok claims that the modern term 'semiotic,' introduced by Locke, corresponds to the Greek *semeiotike*, which is derived from *semeiotikos*. It has been pointed out to me by Robert Hahn, however, that the term '*semeiotike*' cannot be found in extant classical writings. Luigi Romeo in 'The Derivation of "Semiotics" through the History of the Discipline,' *Semeoisis* 6 (1977): 37-49, accounts for this by speculating that Locke's term is instead derived from the Medieval *semeiotice*, a term then mistakenly assigned by Renaissance lexicographers as corresponding to a Greek noun.

2 The principal ones are *Against the Logicians (Adversos Mathematicos)* and *Outlines of Pyrrhonism* in *Sextus Empiricus*, by R.G. Bury, Loeb Classical Library, Cambridge, Mass., Harvard University Press, 4 vols., 1949-57.

3 *Prognostic*, 1, 1-8 in *Hippocrates*, trans. by W.H.S. Jones, Loeb Classical Library, Cambridge, Mass., Harvard University Press, 19231, Vol. II.

4 *Institutio Oratoria*, Bk. V, Ch. IX. See *The Institute Oratoria of Marcus Fabius Quintiliamus*, trans. by C. Little, Nashville, George Peabody College for Teachers, 1951, Vol. I.

5 *Rhetorica*, 1357b18. Translation by W. Rhys Roberts in R. McKeon (ed.), *The Basic Works of Aristotle*, New York, Random House, 1941.

6 *Against the Logicians*, II, 245.

7 ibid., 253. See also VII, 245, 358, 364-7.

8 ibid., 264. In this and the quotation which follows Sextus is not simply presenting but defending the Epicurean view.

9 ibid., 269-71. Note that the first example of a sign interpreted by a lower animal, the footprint, stands for an object, while the second, the prod or the crack of the whip, stands for an action. For the latter Sextus reports that there is a 'must' or 'ought' conclusion.

10 ibid., II, 188 and VIII, 215ff. The argument is presented by Charlotte Stough in *Greek Skepticism*, Berkeley, University of California Press, 1969, pp. 97-137. Stough points out that Sextus's argument is anticipated by the Greek skeptic philosopher Aenesidemus. See also C.K. Ogden and I.A Richards, *The Meaning of Meaning*, New York, Harcourt & Brace, 1923, Appendix C.

11 Fragment VIII, 1-5 and Fragment XIX as translated by Leonardo Taran in *Parmenides*, Princeton, Princeton University Press, 1965.

12 *Against the Logicians*, VIII, 200.

13 *De Interpretatione*, 16a1-7. Translation by H.G. Apostle in *Aristotle's Categories and Propositions*, Grinnell, Peripatetic Press, 1980. The bracketed Greek words are mine; the bracketed expressions in English are Apostle's.

14 See *Semiotics and the Philosophy of Language*, pp. 27-9. Eco concludes that Aristotle's use of *semeia* to stand for words is only 'incidental.'

15 But the extent of Augustine's originality has been a subject of controversy. R.A. Markus emphasizes this originality, noting that the early Christian writers applied the term '*signum*' to Scriptural events and biblical miracles. In the period before Augustine (with the possible exceptions of Plotinus), concludes Markus, 'for no writer is the theory of signs primarily a theory of language, nor is reflection on language carried on in terms of "signs".' See 'St. Augustine on Signs' in Markus (ed.), *Augustine: A Collection of Critical Essays*, New York, Doubleday, 1972. B.D. Jackson claims to find more similarities between Augustine's theory and the Stoic theory of evidence, and claims the Stoics as anticipating Augustine's view. See 'The Theory of Signs in St. Augustine's *De Doctrina Christiana*' in this same collection.

16 *De Dialecta*, V, 9-10. Translated by B.D. Jackson in *Augustine: De Dialecta*, Dordrecht, Reidel, 1975.

17 *De Doctrina Christiana*, II, 2, 12-15. Translation by Jackson in 'The Theory of Signs in St. Augustine's *De Doctrina Christiana*.'

18 ibid., 3, 1-6. Translation again by Jackson.

19 ibid., 24, 37. The contrast between the intentional and conventional aspects in Augustine's characterization is noted by Jackson. Markus, in 'St. Augustine on Signs,' regards the conventional aspects as essential for *signa data*, for he excludes from this category facial expressions and 'sounds whereby animals communicate to one another their desires, their perceptions of food or dangers and so forth.'

20 *De Trinitate*, XV, 10, 18. Translated by Markus in 'St. Augustine on Signs.' Thomas Mitchell has pointed out to me that a similar view can be found in the writings of Aquinas. In his *De Differentia Verbi Divini et Humani*, Sec. 287, we find: 'It is clear, nevertheless, that that which is signified as existing internally in the soul [*illud quod significatur interius in anima existens*] is prior to the word itself that is proffered by the exterior voice [*verbum exteriori voce prolatum*], which is its existing cause.' Later in Section 288 Aquinas says the external word is the 'sign' of the internal word's existence. See Aquinas's *Opuscula Philosophica*, R.M. Spiazzi (ed.), Taurini, Mariett, 1954, p. 101. I owe the translation of this passage to Charles Speck and G.K. Plochmann.

21 William of Ockham, *Super Quatuor Libros Sententarium Subtilissimae Earumdenque Decisiones*, II, qu. 25. Translation by Stephen Tornay in *Ockham: Studies and Sections*, La Salle: Open Court, 1938, p. 19.

22 *Summa Totius Logicae*, Pt. II, Ch. 1. Translation in Tornay, pp. 92, 93.

23 ibid. For an exposition of Ockham's views see Gordon Leff, *William*

of Ockham, Manchester, Manchester University Press, 1975, pp. 42, 43.

24 How thorough-going is the shift in focus towards language is shown by the curious inversion of the classical evidential sign noted by Ian Hacking in *The Emergence of Probability*, London, Cambridge University Press, 1975, pp. 42, 43. The primary evidence became in the Middle Ages the testimony of some source, with the authority of this source determining the reliability of the evidence. Hacking points out how natural events then came to be regarded as God's testimony to man, and the interpretation of these events as natural signs was regarded as the task of giving a correct reading of nature as God's 'Book.' It has been pointed out to me by G.K. Plochmann that St Bonaventure regards creatures as 'shadows' and 'traces' from which God's nature can be inferred. See his *Commentary on the Four Books of Sentences of Peter Lombard*, Pt. I, Qu. II, trans. by R. McKeon in *Selections from Medieval Philosophers*, Vol. II, New York, Scribner's, 1930.

25 *Elements of Philosophy*, Pt. I, Ch. 2, 2.

26 *Essay Concerning the Human Understanding*, Bk. IV, Ch. XXI, Sec. 4.

27 Antoine Arnauld, *The Art of Thinking* [*L'Art de Penser*], First Discourse, Pt. I, Ch. 4. Translation by J. Dickhoff and P. James, Indianapolis, Bobbs Merrill, 1964.

28 Thomas Reid, *An Inquiry into the Human Mind*, Pt. II, Ch. 5, Sec. III.

29 ibid., Pt. II, Ch. 4, Sec. II. The passages that follow are also from this section.

30 *Three Dialogues between Hylas and Philonous*, I.

31 C. Hartshorne and P. Weiss (eds), *The Collected Papers of Charles Sanders Peirce*, 6 vols., Cambridge, Mass., 1934-36, 2.227.

32 ibid., 2.228.

33 ibid., 2.231. Shortly after this passage Peirce offers as an example the sentence 'That vessel there carries no freight at all, but only passengers' as uttered by someone to a hearer who is looking at the vessel being referred to.

34 The other category is that of icons. Peirce also has a more complex classification of signs in which they are sub-divided into 64 classes by a formal scheme that follows his metaphysical categories of firstness, secondness, and thirdness. See 2.234-42.

35 ibid., 2.248. He also gives as an example the rolling gait of a man as a 'probable indication that he is a sailor' (2.285), where the index is a classical evidential sign but not a causal effect.

36 The bullet hole, Peirce says, would be an index of the bullet 'whether anybody has the sense to attribute it to a shot or not' (2.304).

37 ibid., 2.288.

38 ibid., 2.249.

39 The crack of the whip as a sign of an action would seem to be the

object of what Peirce refers to as 'dynamic' or 'energetic' interpretation. See *Collected Papers*, 4.536 and 5.475.

40 ibid., 2.292.

41 ibid., 5.476. As George Gentry notes, this view of the sign's interpretant as a habit is a later view of Peirce's; in earlier versions the interpretant of a sign is always another sign. See 'Habit and the Logical Interpretant' in P. Weiner and F. Young (eds), *Studies in the Philosophy of Charles Sanders Peirce*, Cambridge, Mass., Harvard University Press, 1952.

42 *Course in General Linguistics*, trans. by W. Baskin, New York, Philosophical Library, rev. ed., 1974, Intro., Ch. III.

43 Pierre Guiraud, *Semiology*, trans. by G. Gross, London, Routledge & Kegan Paul, 1975, p. 22.

44 For a review of other contributions to semiology in the Saussurean tradition, including those of Buyssens, Hjelmslev, and Uldall, see Sebeok, *Contributions to the Doctrine of Signs*, pp. 17-21.

45 Roland Barthes, *Elements of Semiology*, trans. by A. Lavers and C. Smith, New York, Hill and Wang, 1967, pp. 11-15. British and American writers sometimes use the term 'semiotics' of Barthes's extended study of cultural forms. For a good review of the contributions of Barthes and other Continental writers see Kaja Silverman, *The Subject of Semiotics*, New York, Oxford University Press, 1983.

46 C.K. Ogden and I.A. Richards, *The Meaning of Meaning*, New York, Harcourt & Brace, 1923, pp. 139, 140.

47 This extension is made by J.B. Watson for whom 'words function in the matter of calling out responses exactly as did the objects for which the words serve as substitutes.' See his *Behaviorism*, New York, Norton, 1925, p. 233. A similar theory is developed by Bertrand Russell in *An Inquiry into Meaning and Truth*, London, Allen & Unwin, 1940. 'When you hear an object-word which you understand,' Russell says, 'your behavior is, up to a point, that which the object itself would have caused. This may occur . . . by the ordinary rules of conditioned reflexes, since the word has become associated with the object' (p. 68).

48 See C.E. Osgood, 'On Understanding and Creating Sentences,' *American Psychology*, 18, 1963: 735-51 and Osgood, G. Succi, and P. Tannenbaum, 'The Logic of Semantic Differentiation' in S. Saporta (ed.), *Psycholinguistics*, New York, Holt Rinehart & Winston 1965.

49 See especially Roger Brown, *Words and Things*, Glencoe, Free Press, 1958, pp. 93ff.

50 The precise definition given in *Signs, Language and Behavior*, New York, Braziller, 1946, p. 10, is as follows: 'If anything A, is a preparatory-stimulus which in the absence of stimulus-objects initiating response-sequences of a certain behavior-family causes a disposition in some organism to respond under certain conditions by response-sequences of this behavior family, then A is a sign.'

51 ibid., pp. 13, 18. Morris's early theory can be found in *Foundations of the Theory of Signs*, Vol. I of O. Neurath (ed.), *International Encyclopedia of Unified Science*, Chicago, University of Chicago Press, 1938, and seems to be a version of the direct response theory. For criticisms of this version see C.J. Ducasse, 'Some Comments on C.W.Morris's 'Foundations of the Theory of Signs',' *Journal of Philosophy and Phenomenological Research*, 3 (1942): 43-52.

52 See Rudolph Carnap, 'Meaning and Synonymy in Natural Languages,' Appendix D of *Meaning and Necessity*, Chicago, University of Chicago Press, 1947.

53 W.V.O. Quine, *Word and Object*, Cambridge, Mass., MIT Press, 1960, pp. 26-40.

54 Even for Quine's linguistic version there are difficulties in identifying the types of stimuli required for the definition of meaning. For a discussion of the difficulties in making the interpersonal comparisons required for translation see D. Follesdal, 'Meaning and Experience' in S. Guttenplana (ed.), *Mind and Language*, Oxford, Clarendon Press, 1974.

55 Roderick Chisholm, 'Intentionality and the Theory of Signs,' *Philosophical Studies*, 3, 1952: 56-63. Chisholm's criticisms are directed towards Carnap's version of the dispositional theory, and are here reformulated to apply to Quine's. Translations of the alien language into the linguist's language Quine regards as fallible empirical hypotheses, and hence he can admit (and has admitted) the difficulties Chisholm raises. Nevertheless, these difficulties serve to throw into question the basic definitions of meaning that are central to his theory. For criticisms directed specifically against Quine's theory see Noam Chomsky, 'Quine's Empirical Assumptions' in D. Davidson and J. Hintikka (eds), *Words and Objections*, Boston, Reidel, 1969.

56 This application is made by Friedrich Waismann in *Principles of Linguistic Philosophy*, London, Macmillan, 1965, p. 13: 'By means of words grouped and combined in different ways we can move the limbs of other people as with invisible strings or wires, and in this way direct their actions. In the last analysis there is nothing there except the signs and their effect; so the effect must be its meaning.'

57 *Verbal Behavior*, New York, Appleton-Century-Crofts, 1957, p. 84.

58 Thomas Sebeok, *Contributions to the Doctrine of Signs*, pp. 65, 66 and *Approaches to Semiotic*, The Hague, Mouton, 1964, pp. 277-87. Note the plural 's' in Sebeok's 'semiotics'. It seems appropriate because Sebeok seems to apply both 'zoosemiotics' and 'anthroposemiotics' to the collection of those empirical sciences having a common subject matter.

59 Though Sebeok notes in *Contributions to the Doctrine of Signs*, p. 49 that the term '*Semiotik*' until quite recently was also applied in Germany to the diagnosis of medical symptoms.

60 G. Harman, 'Semiotics and the Cinema' in G. Mast and M. Cohen

(eds), *Film Theory and Criticism*, London, Oxford University Press, 1979. I have replaced Harman's italics with quotes to indicate mentioned expressions. In *Semiotics and the Philosophy of Language*, p. 19, Eco replies to Harman by appealing to the 2,000 years of tradition of semiotics. This is, of course, in itself unconvincing, since it is entirely possible that this tradition was based on a misconception.
61 See Buhler's 'The Axiomatization of the Language Sciences' in R. Innis, *Karl Buhler: Semiotic Foundations of Language Theory*, New York, Plenum Press, 1982.
62 Chomsky, 'The General Properties of Language' in F.L. Daley (ed.), *Brain Mechanisms Underlying Speech and Language*, New York, Grune and Stratton, 1967.
63 See his 'Review of Skinner's *Verbal Behavior*,' *Language*, 35, 1959: 25-58.
64 J.L. Austin, 'Truth' in J.O. Urmson and G.J. Warnock (eds), *Philosophical Papers*, Oxford, Clarendon Press, 1961.
65 *Signs, Language and Behavior*, p. 33.
66 ibid., p. 17. 'Anything which would permit the completion of the response-sequences to which the interpreter is disposed because of a sign,' Morris says, 'will be called the *denotatum* of the sign. A sign will be said to *denote* a denotatum.'

3 Natural signs

1 The boulder example is from William Alston's *Philosophy of Language*, Eaglewood, Prentice-Hall, 1964, p. 50.
2 But if we identify emotional states with brain states these items of behavior can be claimed to be symptoms and causal effects of these states, not criteria. This position is argued for by Hilary Putnam in 'Brains and Behavior' in R.J. Butler (ed.), *Analytical Philosophy*, Vol. 2, Oxford, Blackwell, 1965. Establishing the identities, however, would seem to require first independently identifying the emotional states, and for this behavior would certainly seem criterial and not a contingent effect.
3 H.H. Price *Thinking and Experience*, Cambridge, Mass., Harvard University Press, 1953, p. 106.
4 The example is given by Kenneth Friedman in 'Analysis of Causality in Terms of Determinism,' *Mind*, 89 (1980): 544-64. The relation is non-causal, Friedman argues, because the metabolic rate is not also a necessary condition for the rising pressure: suppressing the former does not eliminate the latter.
5 *Collected Papers*, 2.286.
6 I follow our ordinary ways of speaking of objects and states of affairs as well as events as being the relata of the cause-effect relation. Thus, the presence of boulders, fossils, and spots is said to be the effect of past glaciers, life forms, and present measles.
7 'Semiologie et Médecine' in R. Bastide (ed.), *Les Sciences de la*

Folie, Paris, Mouton, 1972.

8 See Sebeok, *Contributions to the Doctrine of Signs*, pp. 126, 127.

9 Eco, *Semiotic and the Philosophy of Language*, pp. 36-43. A similar error is made by Andrew Jones in *Communication and Meaning*, Dordrecht, Reidel, 1983, where he compares a person's regular walking habits as a sign of the time of day to a conventional signal such as the hanging of a lantern in Boston as a sign the British were coming. Jones says he has 'no hesitation in assigning truth conditions to actions' such as the regular walking (p.14).

10 It would not be accurate to claim that these signs constituted the extension of *'semeion'* for the Epicureans, who it will be recalled from 2.1 cited sign interpretation by lower animals in their attempt to refute the Stoic inferential theory. By retaining the examples of the classical evidential signs and including medical symptoms they clearly did not intend our restriction. Nevertheless, the Epicureans provide an anticipation of the view defended here.

11 Signs of the kind characterized here seem to be what Ogden and Richards in *The Meaning of Meaning* refer to as 'initial signs:' 'Directly apprehended retinal modifications such as colors are therefore *initial* signs of "objects" and "events"' (p. 82). They cite with approval Helmholtz's view that 'sensations which lie at the basis of all perceptions are subjective signs of external objects' (p. 79).

12 In *Sense and Sensibilia*, G.L. Warnock (ed.), Oxford, Clarendon Press, 1962 and *Concept of Mind*, New York, Barnes & Noble, 1949, Ch. VI. See also Richard Rorty, *Philosophy and the Mirror of Nature*, Princeton, Princeton University Press, 1979 for an exposition and criticism of this theory that dominated post-Cartesian philosophy.

13 For the opposing view that mirror images are representations see Virgil Aldrich, 'Mirrors, Pictures, Words, Perceptions,' *Philosophy*, 55 (1980): 39-56. Aldrich does concede, however, 'that any x in the role of representing y tends to function simply as a point of view on y, or to disappear in favor of the y it intends.' This disappearance of the image, he says, 'makes the question of their resemblance slippery.'

14 See Kendall Walton, 'Transparent Pictures: The Nature of Photographic Realism' and Fred Dretske, 'Seeing Through Pictures,' both in *Nous*, 18 (1984): 67-74. The issue defined by Walton is whether photos are 'transparent' (we see objects by means of them) or 'opaque' (we see photos as representations of objects). Dretske argues that photos are natural signs, and includes TV images also within this category: 'In watching a football game on television . . . we get information about the game by getting information about what is on the television screen' (p. 74). The screen image, he concludes, is 'informationally' but not 'perceptually' transparent. A version of Dretske's view is presented (and eventually rejected) by Max Black in 'How Do Pictures Represent?' in E.H. Gombrich, J. Hochberg,

and M. Black, *Art, Perception, and Reality*, Baltimore, Johns Hopkins University Press, 1972. On this view, says Black, a photograph P is regarded as a 'trace' of the object it depicts, and 'the interpretation of P is a matter of inference to an earlier time in a causal sequence.'

15 E.M. Gombrich calls a photograph a 'natural trace, a series of tracks left . . . on the emulsion of the film by the variously distributed light waves which produced chemical changes made visible and permanent.' See his 'The Evidence of Images' in S. Singleton (ed.), *Interpretation, Theory and Practice*, Baltimore, Johns Hopkins Press, 1969. It is, however, not normally interpreted as a trace (though it could be) by one who views it, unlike Peirce's indices.

16 This Wittgensteinian notion of 'showing' as contrasted with 'saying' is applied to photos by Black in 'How Do Pictures Represent?'.

17 Certainly the showing relation between image and object cannot be explained in terms of resemblance between the two. For criticisms of such an explanation for pictures that can be extended to material images see Nelson Goodman, *The Languages of Art*, Indianapolis, Hacket, 1956, pp. 3-12.

18 For singular sentences complete interpretation thus coincides with what is called 'verification' and 'falsification.' For generalizations, whether uniform or statistical, conducting at least one experimental test constitutes complete interpretation in the sense intended here, even though acceptance or rejection of the generalization may not result.

19 Morris, for example, writes of the food found by the dog as what is 'denoted' by the buzzer. The denotatum of the sign, he says, is 'anything which would permit the completion of the response-sequences to which the interpreter is disposed because of a sign,' in contrast to its significance (or 'significatum'), which is 'those conditions which are such that whatever fulfills them is a denotatum.' See *Signs, Language and Behavior*, pp. 17, 18. Peirce's triadic relation of sign, interpretant, and object seems to assume a referential relation between every sign to some object for its interpreter. Over and over again we find this error perpetuated in the semiotic tradition following Peirce in the form of diagrams with arrows pointing from sign to an object representing what is taken as a referential relation.

20 The contrast to Morris's views should again be noted. In *Signs, Language and Behavior* signs are said to be 'true' 'in so far as they correctly determine the expectations of their users' (p. 33). But in the absence of a conventional rule there is no sense to a 'correct' determination. Morris describes a sign as 'reliable' 'to the degree that it denotes in the various instances of its appearance. If an animal always found food at a certain place when a buzzer sounded the buzzer would be completely reliable.' (p. 106). Here again terminology is misapplied. For *us* a sign can be reliable in the sense that

it is supported by a generalization with high probability and speakers can be more or less reliable depending on our confirmation of what they have to say. But at the level of natsigns 'reliable' has no application.

21 P.F. Strawson, *The Bounds of Sense*, London, Methuen, 1966, p. 273.

22 This recognition as well as sign discrimination seems to be what Jonathan Bennett includes under the heading of what he calls 'registration' in *Linguistic Behavior*, Cambridge, Cambridge University Press, 1976, p. 46. Registration, he says, is a 'perceptual or epistemic matter' which depends on whether goal-seeking behavior is modified. Our observation of this modification may be our only means of identifying registration in lower animals, but it seems possible for there to be registration without behavior change.

23 Peirce also distinguishes what he terms the 'emotional interpretant' of a sign. Emotional interpretation can be regarded as a third mode in which the sign's significance evokes an emotional attitude on the part of its interpreter, whether that of fear or hope, aversion or wanting. Thus, the sight of the candle signifies intense heat to which a person's attitude is that of fear or aversion. In the discussion that follows we assimilate this mode to dynamic interpretation. For higher-level signs it is easier to distinguish it, but since signs as objects of this interpretation seem to display no unique logical functions we ignore emotional interpretation in later chapters.

Our cognitive-dynamic contrast corresponds also to H.H. Price's distinction between the 'cognitive aspect' of significance and the 'practical' aspect. For the former, Price says, X is the sign *of* Y; for the latter X is the sign *for* an action taken in order to secure or avoid Y. See *Thinking and Experience*, pp. 91ff.

24 For a more complete account of both forms of inference see my *Practical Inferences*, Routledge & Kegan Paul, 1985, pp. 15-22, 51-5.

25 See Saul Kripke, 'A Puzzle About Belief' in A. Margalit (ed.), *Meaning and Use*, Dordrecht, D. Reidel, 1976.

26 The inapplicability of belief ascriptions to non-language users is noted by Davidson in 'Thought and Talk' in S. Guttenplan (ed.), *Mind and Language*, Oxford, Clarendon Press, 1975. But he draws the more general conclusion that 'thoughts' cannot be ascribed to those without linguistic capacity. This more general denial of any psychological ascriptions other than feelings or sensations seems mistaken.

27 See Ralph Barton Perry's distinction between signs as 'representative stimuli' whose interpretation is based on prior learning and stimuli triggering instinctive behavior in *General Theory of Value*, New York, Longman, 1926, pp. 177-9.

4 Communication

1 The term 'comsign' is borrowed from Charles Morris who assigns it a somewhat different meaning. What Morris, following G.H. Mead, calls a 'gesture' is a non-conventional sign used to communicate, e.g. the snarl of a dog. Only when a gesture 'has the same effect on the individual making it that it has on the individual to whom it is addressed' does it become for Mead a 'significant symbol.' Significant symbols are said to 'have the same meaning for all individual members of [a] given society or social group.' See *Mind, Self and Society*, C.W. Morris (ed.), Chicago, University of Chicago Press, 1934, pp. 46, 47. Mead's significant symbol is what Morris terms a comsign in 'Foundations of the Theory of Signs,' p. 36. It proves convenient, however, to take 'comsign' in a generic sense that contrasts its extension with that of natsigns and then distinguish within the class of comsigns conventional comsigns, signs which coincide with Mead's significant symbols, and non-conventional comsigns which include Mead's gestures. The bristling-snarling example that follows is used by Mead to illustrate the contrast between a movement by an animal and a vocal gesture.

2 See 'Meaning,' *Philosophical Review*, 66 (1957): 377–88. 'Comsign' is preferable to 'utterance' because of its more natural application to gestures and other means of non-verbal communication. For the same reasons I replace Grice's 'utterer' by 'communicator' and 'audience' by 'interpreter'. The generality achieved allows the extension of Grice's analysis to the examples of lower animal communication discussed below.

3 The policeman standing in the way of the motorist is, of course, not evidence from which to infer some other fact, but instead a circumstance from which to infer by way of a practical inference. Cf. 3.4.

4 The original counterexamples are by Strawson in 'Intention and Convention in Speech Acts,' *Philosophical Review*, 73 (1964): 439–60 and John Searle in *Speech Acts*, Cambridge, Cambridge University Press, 1969, pp. 43–50. Perhaps the most sophisticated later elaboration is by Stephen Schiffer in *Meaning*, Oxford, Oxford University Press, 1974, p. 63. Simon Blackburn proposes that to avoid deception we simply add the additional condition that the communicator intends that all his intentions be recognized, thus ensuring what he calls 'openness.' See his *Spreading the Word*, Oxford, Clarendon Press, 1984, p. 116. A similar solution is proposed by Jonathan Bennett in *Linguistic Behavior*, Cambridge, Cambridge University Press, 1976, p. 127.

5 Strawson, 'Convention and Intention in Speech Acts,' p. 460. In Austin's terminology no specific perlocutionary effect may be intended, though the speaker must intend his utterance to have some illocutionary force.

6 That belief as an effect is not necessary is noted by H.L.A. Hart in 'Signs and Words,' *Philosophical Quarterly*, 2 (1952): 59-62.
7 In *Biological Bases of Human Social Behavior*, New York, McGraw-Hill, 1974, p. 114.
8 E.W. Menzel, Jr, 'Communication About the Environment in a Group of Young Chimpanzees,' *Folia Primatologica*, 15 (1971): 220-32.
9 Hinde, *Biological Bases*, p. 114.
10 ibid., p. 115. The low gutteral bark of a chimpanzee reinforced by turning and playing is offered as an example. Some philosophers have ruled out ascribing intentions to lower animals on logical grounds. Thus Stuart Hampshire in *Thought and Action*, London, Chatto & Windus, 1959: 'The difference here between a human being and an animal lies in the possibility of the human being expressing his intention and putting into words his intention to do so-and-so. . . . It is a . . . difference . . . correctly expressed as the senselessness of attributing intentions to an animal which has not the means to reflect upon, and to announce to itself or to others, its own future behavior' (p. 98). This seems a totally arbitrary stipulation which is at variance with ways in which we actually describe animal behavior. G.E.M. Anscombe seems closer to this usage when she ascribes intentionality to animals without language in *Intention*, Ithaca, Cornell University Press, 1957, p. 85.
11 W. John Smith, *The Behavior of Communicating*, Cambridge, Mass., Harvard University Press, 1977, p. 264. N. Tinbergen regards almost all signaling behavior as innate and reflex: 'Except perhaps in the highest mammals, all signaling behavior is immediate reaction to internal and external stimuli. In this respect there is a great difference between animals and Man.' See *Social Behavior in Animals*, London, Methuen, 1953, p. 74. A stronger conclusion, and one that does not seem warranted by available evidence, is reached by Bennett. He concludes in *Linguistic Behavior* that animal displays are 'due to the existence in [a] species of certain inflexible, wired-in behavior patterns whose instances do not exhibit intentionalness of any sort' (p. 204).
12 *Biological Bases*, p. 90.
13 See Grice, 'Utterer's Meaning, Sentence-Meaning, and Word-Meaning,' *Foundations of Language*, 4 (1968): 255-42 for a detailed attempt to state the relationships between occasion and timeless meaning.
14 This objection is formulated by Paul Ziff in 'On H.P. Grice's Account of Meaning,' *Analysis*, 28 (1967): 1-8.
15 For a similar view of the role of iconic comsigns and transfers from natsigns such as involuntary cries see Bennett's *Linguistic Behavior*, pp. 140, 141, 206. The historical transition of Chinese written characters from iconic to non-iconic conventionalized signs is another obvious example of what is being discussed here. The issue of

whether and to what extent human languages initially evolved from a 'natural' iconic link to what is signified is, of course, one much debated by philosophers and linguists. Roger Brown in *Words and Things*, Glencoe, Free Press, 1958, pp. 110ff. cites evidence for a 'phonetic symbolism' for which there is iconic representation between speech sounds and magnitudes.

16 In *Convention*, Cambridge, Mass., Harvard University Press, 1969, p. 42.

17 Exactly such a combination of the two sets of conditions is proposed by Bennett in *Linguistic Behavior*, pp. 177-9.

18 See Paul Ziff, *Semantic Analysis*, Ithaca, Cornell University Press, 1960, pp. 42ff. Such correlations are termed 'conditional regularities' by Schiffer in *Meaning*, p. 155, where he summarizes Lewis's theory.

19 That linguistic semantic conventions are not semantic regularities is argued for by Saul Kripke in stating Wittgenstein's 'skeptical paradox' that arises out of the possible use of two expressions with different conventional meanings, e.g. 'plus' and 'quus' or 'green' and 'grue', where there is no observable difference in linguistic behavior, whether in computing numbers or in applications to colors. It is the practice of mutual correction within the linguistic community that determines the meaning of expressions for Kripke (following Wittgenstein), not simply coincidence of behavior.

20 'Truth' in J.O. Urmson and G.J. Warnock (eds), *Philosophical Papers*, Oxford, Clarendon Press, 1961. I avoid in these discussions the term 'statement' as standing for an object of which 'truth' and 'falsity' are predicated, preferring instead to speak of utterances as being judged true or false, or being assented to or denied.

21 In 'Sceptical Confusions About Rule-Following,' *Mind*, 93 (1984): 423-9.

22 *Contributions to the Doctrine of Signs*, p. 120. Georg Klaus distinguishes a sign as an object of consciousness (*bewustein*) from a signal producing a determinate behavioral effect. See *Semiotik und Erkenntsnistheorie*, Berlin, Deutscher Verlag der Wissenschaften, 1969, pp. 55ff. Suzanne Langer contrasts signals as 'substitute stimuli' evoking responses normally evoked by objects for which they are being substituted from symbols which 'are not proxy for their objects, but are vehicles for the conception of objects' in *Philosophy in a New Key*, Cambridge, Mass., Harvard University Press, 1951, p. 61. Our use of 'signal' shares many features with Peirce's 'rheme' (*Collected Papers*, 2.272), and it is tempting to use Peirce's term as a way of avoiding associations of 'signal'. But in a discipline where artificial terminology is overly abundant, it seems more advisable to choose the more familiar term and run the risk of its mechanistic associations. Also, Peirce's rheme is a sign of 'qualitative possibility' (cf. 2.250), and this would seem to rule out applying it, as we do here, to proper names.

23 *Biological Bases of Human Social Behavior*, p. 83.

24 For the contrast between the information of a 'signal sequence' and 'semantic information' see Yehoshua Bar-Hillel, *Language and Information*, Cambridge, Mass., MIT Press, 1964, pp. 275-97.

25 See *Signs, Language and Behavior*, p. 58.

26 Cf. Quine, *Word and Object*, pp. 94, 95 for an account of the transition from recognizing Mama-like features to recognizing Mama as an individual.

27 'Teleology and the Great Shift,' *Journal of Philosophy*, 81 (1984): 647-53. De Sousa formulates his distinction in terms of goal-directed behavior; I reformulate it here in terms of sign interpretation.

28 Cf. W.J. Smith, *The Behavior of Communicating*, pp. 59, 60. Smith cites studies of animal calls among species as diverse as chickadees, elephant seals, and reindeers in support of conclusions about signatures for animal communication. Long-distance communication with signatures can be accomplished also by chemical transmission, e.g. female sex pheromones which inhibit the approach of members of other species. Badges found in certain animal species, e.g. bird plumage indicating species, sex, and even mating availability, though they are of course not intentionally produced, can be regarded as primitive precursors of addresses.

29 All but the third and sixth features outlined are included in C.F. Hockett's list of 'design features' for communication systems. See his 'Logical Considerations in the Study of Animal Communication' in W.E. Lanyon and W.N. Tavolga (eds), *Animal Sounds and Communication*, Washington, D.C., American Institute of Biological Sciences, 1960 and C.F. Hockett and S.A. Altmann, 'A Note on Design Features' in T. Sebeok (ed.), *Animal Communication*, Bloomington, Indiana University Press, 1968. In the latter work altogether sixteen features are listed. In 'The Problem of Universals in Language' in J.H. Greenberg (ed.), *Universals of Language*, 2nd ed., Cambridge, Mass., MIT Press, 1966 Hockett lists duality of patterning, displacement, and openness, the capacity to generate infinitely many signs, as the three features whose joint presence is most important for distinguishing human languages from animal signal systems.

30 The possibility of complex signals for animal communication is raised in A.M. Wenner, 'The Study of Animal Communication' in Sebeok and Ramsay (eds), *Approaches to Animal Communication*, The Hague, Mouton, 1957.

31 Hockett in 'Logical Considerations in the Study of Animal Communication' speculates that bird songs may exhibit the second level of patterning, while Wenner raises the possibility of a signaling system exhibiting the first level in 'The Study of Animal Communication.' Diebold speculates that of all the sixteen design features listed by Hockett and Altmann only duality of patterning is unique to human languages in 'Anthropological Perspectives' in Sebeok (ed.), *Animal Communication*.

32 With syntactic rules for forming sentences comes also the possibility of sentence embedding and the formation of relative clauses and prepositional phrases. The formulation of these rules for given languages is the topic of transformational grammar as presented originally in Chomsky's *Syntactic Structures*, The Hague, Mouton, 1957.

33 In 'Logical Considerations in the Study of Animal Communication' Hockett cites this dance as the unique case of displacement occurring without language. But this is because he uses 'displacement' in the behavioral sense of orienting towards distant objects, not in the interpretive sense of enabling extension of a referent occasion.

5 Language

1 See *Signs, Language and Behavior*, p. 36.

2 The combination of nucleus with qualifiers is what Otto Jespersen calls a 'junction,' in contrast to the combination of 'nexus' connecting subjects with predicates. A junction, he says, is a 'unit or single idea, expressed more or less accidentally by means of two elements', while a nexus 'always contains two ideas which must remain separate.' See *The Philosophy of Grammar*, London, Allen & Unwin, 1924, p. 116.

3 Roman Jakobson notes how 'decisively important' is the capacity to use subject–predicate sentences in the child's development: 'It liberates speech from the here and now and enables the child to treat events distant in time and space or even fictitious.' See his 'Verbal Communication,' *Scientific American*, 227 (1972): 73-80. R.M. Yerkes cites an experiment that seems to illustrate the different psychological capacities of interpreters of signals and sentences. A chimpanzee can be shown food put in one of four differently colored boxes, but if their positions are interchanged it will not be able to discriminate between the boxes and find the food after a delay. It will find the food, however, if the positions of the boxes remain unchanged. Thus, lower animals seem capable of delayed reactions relating a *place* to a kind of object (the food), but only humans as interpreters of sentences seem to relate one kind of object (a colored box) to another kind. See R.M. Yerkes, *Chimpanzees, A Laboratory Colony*, New Haven, Yale University Press, 1943.

4 We are restricting ourselves here to what Quine calls *occasion sentences*, sentences whose truth or falsity varies with occasion of utterance. These are contrasted to *standing sentences*, general sentences such as 'All crows are black' whose truth values are at least relatively independent of this occasion. See *Word and Object*, pp. 35, 36.

5 The view that temporal determination belongs logically in the subject term is argued for by Bolzano. It is a given object A at time to which we ascribe an attribute b, says Bolzano, not an attribute b at t which we ascribed to A: 'It does not happen at time t that the attribute b is

claimed for the object A; but the object A, inasmuch as it is thought
to exist at time t (hence to have this determination) is claimed to
have attribute b.' See his *Theory of Science*, trans. by R. George,
Oxford, Blackwell, 1972.

6 See O.H. Mowrer, 'The Psychologist Looks at Language' in
L. Jakobovits and M. Miron (eds), *Readings in the Psychology of
Language*, Englewood Cliffs, Prentice-Hall, 1967, for an attempt to
provide a behavioral account of this meaning transference from
predicates to subjects. For 'Tom is a thief', says Mowrer, the
meaning of 'thief' gets transferred to that of 'Tom' in such a way that
our response to Tom is modified.

7 It is also sufficient to refute Kant's formulation of the analytic-
synthetic distinction. For Kant a sentence of the form 'All *S* is *P*' is
analytic if *P* is used as a criterion for identifying individuals as an S,
or in Kant's terms if *P* is 'part of the meaning' of *S*. But if *P* expresses
a criterion for an S based on prior acceptance of what was false, then
'All *S* is *P*' is itself false, and hence not analytic.

8 Jespersen notes how verbs like 'rain' and 'snow' were originally used
without subjects, and then later pronoun subjects were added in the
evolution of language to conform to the grammatical requirement for
a subject. See *The Philosophy of Grammar*, p. 25.

9 See footnote 27 of Chapter 4.

10 Cf. Strawson, *Individuals*, London, Methuen, 1959, pp. 208ff. When
criteria for identification are associated, nouns become capable of
functioning as general subjects having what Strawson calls 'divided
reference' to a plurality of objects.

11 Peirce includes portraits with names within his category of signs
having subject–predicate structure, contrasting them with portraits
without names as 'icons.' See *Collected Papers*, 2.320. See also
E.M. Gombrich, *Art and Illusion*, London, Phaedon Press, 4th ed.,
1972, p. 59 for the view that a picture itself is never true or false, but
can become so when it is accompanied by a label or caption.

12 For this denotation-reference distinction see L.J. Cohen, 'Geach's
Problem About Intentional Identity,' *Journal of Philosophy*, 65
(1968): 329-35. For the same distinction see also Keith Donnellan,
'Speaker Reference, Descriptions, and Anaphora' in P. French and
H. Wettstein (eds), *Contemporary Perspectives in the Philosophy of
Language*, Minneapolis, University of Minnesota Press, 1979.

13 Searle, 'Proper Names,' *Mind*, 67 (1958): 166-73.

14 Saul Kripke, 'Naming and Necessity' in Davidson and Harman (eds),
Semantics of Natural Language. A proper name is for Kripke a 'rigid
designator' designating the same individual in all possible worlds in
contrast to definite descriptions which designate an individual in some
but not all worlds. I ignore here Kripke's application of this
distinction to modal logic except to note that possible worlds seem
invoked to preserve the dyadic denotation relation for definite
descriptions.

15 This theory is outlined in Kripke's 'Naming and Necessity.'
16 I have in mind here only the referential use of a subject of an isolated sentence in contrast to what Donnellan calls an 'attributive use' of a subject in 'Reference and Definition Descriptions,' *Philosophical Review*, 75 (1966): 281-304. An attributive use approximates to the conditions for logical denotation, since it presupposes a narrative context in which predicates P_1, P_2, . . . , P_n are ascribed. The subject term then becomes the definite description 'whoever (whatever) satisfies '$P_1 + P_2 + \ldots + P_n$'.
17 P.T. Geach, 'Assertion,' *Philosophical Review*, 74 (1965): 449-65.
18 That subject negation exists was first pointed out to me by Geoffrey Nathan. I have argued these points at greater length in my 'Negating the Subject,' *Philosophical Studies*, 43 (1980): 349-53.
19 *Philosophical Investigations*, trans. by G.E.M. Anscombe, New York, Macmillan, 1953, Section 304.
20 Perhaps the clearest statement of this relation between meaning and truth conditions is in Davidson's 'Truth and Meaning' and 'The Method of Truth in Metaphysics,' both in *Inquiries into Truth and Interpretation*, Oxford, Clarendon Press, 1984. In the second of these papers Davidson says that a 'theory of truth' must 'show us how we can view each of a potential infinity of sentences as composed from a finite stock of semantically significant atoms (roughly, words) by means of a finite number of applications of a finite number of rules of composition. It must then give the truth conditions of each sentence . . . on the basis of its composition.' That stating truth conditions has the effect of providing a synonymous paraphrase is argued by Dummett in 'What is a Theory of Meaning?' in S. Guttenplan (ed.), *Mind and Language*, Oxford, Clarendon Press, 1975.
21 See his 'Davies on Recent Theories of Metaphor,' *Mind*, 93 (1984): 433-9. Cooper raises the doubt whether any sentence meanings 'are computable on the basis of the meanings of their parts and modes of combination *alone*.'
22 See A. Tarski, 'The Concept of Truth in Formalized Languages' in *Logic, Semantics, Metamathematics*, Oxford, Clarendon Press, 1956. This formula becomes the basis for the theory of meaning developed by Davidson in 'Truth and Meaning.'
23 See J.L. Austin, *How to Do Things with Words*, Cambridge, Mass., Harvard University Press, 1962.
24 Louis Althusser calls this a kind of 'hailing,' in effect saying to another 'Hey, you there!'. See his *Lenin and Philosophy*, trans. by B. Brewster, London, Monthly Review Press, 1971, p. 174.
25 See *The Language of Morals*, Oxford, Oxford University Press, 1952, pp. 17, 18. The imperative shares with the indicative for Hare the common 'phrastic' 'Your closing the door' with subject–predicate structure.
26 See Kant's *Anthropology from a Pragmatic Point of View*, trans. by

V. Dowdell, ed. by H. Rudnick, Carbondale, Southern Illinois University Press, 1978, Bk. I, Sec. 39. Here Kant includes as 'voluntary signs' class signs of hereditary superiority (e.g. coats of arms), uniforms as signs of service, badges of honor (e.g. ribbons), and signs of dishonor such as brandings. This contribution by Kant to semiotic was pointed out to me by Thomas Wilson.

27 Though frequently they function relative to a linguistic background and thus as what we have termed 'post-linguistic' signs.

28 G.E.M. Anscombe, 'The First Person' in S. Guttenplan (ed.), *Mind and Language*. For my amendment to Anscombe's view see my 'The Addressing Function of "I",' *Analysis*, 38 (1978): 91-3.

29 For a summary and criticism of what he calls Wittgenstein's 'no-ownership theory' see Strawson, *Individuals*, London, Methuen, 1959, pp. 95-101. I defend Wittgenstein against these criticisms in 'A Defence of the No-Ownership Theory,' *Mind*, 81 (1972): 97-101. This defense extends only to Wittgenstein's contention that the 'I' in avowals is not used by the speaker as a referring expression.

30 See Strawson, *Individuals*, Chapter 3. See also Sydney Shoemaker, *Self-Knowledge and Self-Identity*, Ithaca, Cornell University Press, 1963 for a defense of Strawson's view. We must postulate the existence of persons as referents of 'I', Shoemaker contends, because of the fact 'that corresponding to any first person statement there are third-person statements that are in a certain sense equivalent to it and certainly 'about something.' So first-person statements must also be about persons' (p. 13).

31 See David Harrah, 'A Logic of Message and Reply,' *Synthese*, 63 (1985): 275-83 for an analysis of a formal memo that distinguishes its 'vector-specifier' from the 'body' of a message conveying information or instructions.

32 The relationship between bivalence and the realist correspondence view is noted by Dummett in 'Truth' and 'Realism', both in *Truth and Other Enigmas*, London, Duckworth, 1978. Instead of the bivalence principle, however, Dummett uses acceptance of the law of excluded middle 'A or not-A' as dividing the realist from the 'anti-realist.' The law follows as a direct consequence of the principle. For a discussion of the bivalence principle and the three-valued logics that result from denying it see my *Deductive Logic*, Carbondale, Southern Illinois University Press, 1974, Section 25.

33 See Quine's 'Two Dogmas of Empiricism' in *From a Logical Point of View*, New York, Harper & Row, 1953.

34 For a defense of the analytic-synthetic distinction see Strawson and Grice, 'In Defense of a Dogma,' *Philosophical Review*, 65 (1956): 141-58. For sentences of the form 'All S is P' where S is a natural kind term (e.g. 'All gold is yellow' or 'All tigers are felines') application of the analytic-synthetic distinction is more difficult, as was noted in footnote 7 of this chapter. For an account of the reference of natural kind terms that has the effect of denying

analyticity for predicates such as 'is yellow' and 'is a feline' see Kripke, 'Naming and Necessity' and Putnam, 'Is Semantics Possible?' in *Mind, Language and Reality*, Cambridge, Cambridge University Press, 1975.

 AME INDEX

SUBJECT INDEX